The Proactive Driver

The Proactive Driver

An Unofficial Guide for All Drivers

Hermann S. Botzow, Jr.

GROVE STREET BOOKS

ISBN: 978-1-94193-401-2
Library of Congress Control Number: 2014955506

Disclaimer

Driving any vehicle safely is the responsibility of the driver. All drivers operate their cars at their own risk. The techniques, suggestions, and ideas contained herein are of broad general usefulness and are not intended to replace actual driving experience, driving skills, or a valid license. Although obtained from reliable sources, the techniques, suggestions, and ideas contained herein cannot be considered absolute recommendations.

Federal, state, local, and other applicable regulations and guidelines concerning road safety and driving practices change frequently. The reader should note, therefore, that the development of new regulations, guidelines, and practices may require changes in some techniques, suggestions, and ideas contained in this material.

Neither the publisher nor the author make any warranty, express or implied, with respect to the use of any techniques, suggestions, and ideas disclosed in this book. The publisher and author disclaim any and all liability for any damage of any kind or character, including without limitation any compensatory, incidental, direct or indirect, special, punitive, or consequential damage, loss of income or profit, loss of or damage to property or person, claims of third parties, or other losses of any kind or character arising out of or in connection with the use of this book or the accuracy of the information contained herein, even if the publisher or author has been advised of the possibility of such damages or losses.

To contact Hermann Botzow, please go to his website:
www.theproactivedriver.com

Book designed by Kirsty Anderson
Cover Design by Henry James
Photograph of author by J. Hildebrandt

Grove Street Books is an imprint of Bauhan Publishing, LLC

Grove Street Books
P.O. Box 117
Peterborough, New Hampshire 03458

www.grovestreetbooks.com

Manufactured in the United States of America

To Tom and Ray Magliozzi,
who have, through their keen intellects and outrageous humor,
converted a generation of unsuspecting Public Radio listeners
into highly observant motorheads.

CONTENTS

Chapter 6 - When You Are Driving 65

Foreword

Several years ago, I watched in abject horror as a pickup truck ran a red light and struck a car crossing an intersection. The pickup impacted the car on the driver's side door. I was stopped at the light headed in the opposite direction of the truck, and the force of the crash flung the crushed car towards me. The car careened to a halt inches from my left front fender with a young mother's body slumped over the wheel. She had been killed instantly. I still shake with helplessness at this completely unnecessary death.

This year over 34,000 other Americans are likely to die in traffic crashes.[1] That is equivalent to the entire population of a small city. These tragic deaths continue to pile up despite our feverish efforts to improve traffic safety. Teen drivers face increasing restrictions, road ragers go to prison, drunks lose their licenses, and the elderly have their eyesight tested. And thus, we continue to nibble away at the deficiencies of relatively small groups of drivers. But the intention of this book is to improve *everyone's* skills.

Previous road safety legislation has helped us already. Seatbelts have saved many lives. Cars are now very comfortable and easy to steer, and they feature a whole host of safety improvements including air bags and antilock brakes. Unfortunately these advances have created a false sense of security that is leading to distracted and extremely dangerous driving practices, such as talking on cell phones and texting.

Meanwhile, today's driver education programs often equip us with only the basic skills needed to pass a driver's test. Over subsequent years, individual drivers may slowly acquire a few advanced skills, but typically on a hit-or-miss basis. What if drivers of all ages and persuasions became aware of the proactive driving skills described in this book? I'm totally convinced that this more comprehensive approach would reduce our annual highway carnage. Imagine, just a 10% reduction would save almost 4,000 lives a year!

From my years of research since that horrible accident, I have concluded that the driver of the pickup truck was the exception rather than the rule. Most of us are already really great defensive drivers who respect our traffic laws. We realize that our lives depend on our driving to protect us from the relatively few red light runners, texting drivers, drunks, and others. And we want as many fellow drivers as possible to become great drivers, because we know that we may someday make a mistake such as rolling through a stop sign. Our transition from defensive drivers to proactive drivers will, hopefully, make all our lives even safer.

Hermann S. Botzow, Jr.
October 2014

Acknowledgments

A number of very caring professionals helped me throughout the lengthy process of researching and writing the manuscript. Greg Benz pounded home the serious and insidious nature of distracted driving such as talking on cell phones and texting. Alan Gonseth shared his extensive knowledge of accident investigation procedures. My long-term mentor, Leon Goodman, brought his wealth of traffic engineering know-how to bear. Dr. Allen Robinson of the American Driver Training and Safety Education Association and Brett Robinson of Highway Safety Services provided a comprehensive overview of Driver Education at the national level. Lindsay Townsend provided me with current thinking in driver education at the state and local level as well as some excellent suggestions for amending the original text. Chester Ludlow introduced me to Vermont's "sidehill" interstates. Jack Bushman contributed ways for good drivers to feel a sense of satisfaction. And Elmo Midgley and Jim Mitchell filled in huge gaps in my knowledge of tractor-trailer operations. Contributions by a whole host of other professionals in the field are identified in the list of references. Judith Hildebrandt corrected the many grammatical and compositional mistakes contained in the early drafts.

Also, I would like to thank both my initial editor, Heather Taylor, and my editor at Grove Street Books, Mary Ann Faughnan, for their enthusiasm and finely honed editing skills. Finally, the book would not have been possible without the outstanding publishing skills of Sarah Bauhan and the other members of her staff, including Henry James for creating the cover and graphic design and Nerissa Osborne for her contributions to the marketing of the book.

Burma-Shave Signs

Chapter 2 and all subsequent chapters begin with a Burma-Shave poem. These verses were introduced in 1925 to advertise a brushless shaving cream and were displayed along major country highways as a series of small red signs with white lettering, the last sign reading, "Burma-Shave." The first of the Burma-Shave safety messages appeared in 1935, and the discovery of a new set of Burma-Shave signs became an eagerly anticipated event for motorists in the 1930s and 1940s. With increased speeds on the interstates, the signs became difficult to read. The last signs disappeared in 1963.

PART 1
BE PROACTIVE, NOT DISTRACTED

CHAPTER 1 – INTRODUCTION

Great Drivers Everywhere

Do you love to drive? A lot of people do. About 200 million.[1] If you grow up in rural America, you know that it is the road in front of your house that leads to the rest of the world. But driving is more than that. It is a way to enjoy our personal freedom. And why not? With the simple observance of a few rules, your car can take you thousands of miles and enable you to perform an infinite variety of tasks.

This book is addressed primarily to drivers who are already licensed. However, newly licensed drivers also can benefit from reading the book. Many of us spend an hour a day in our car driving to and from work. As the years go by, we learn more and more individual driving skills. But what we often lack is an overall philosophy that is the hallmark of proactive drivers. That should interest you. Or, perhaps, some of the many details that the book contains may help you acquire even more advanced driving skills. As my license plate says, we just "LUV-2-DRYV." So, whether you are a recent or seasoned driver, come and join us!

Is there really any need for us to improve? According to a survey of 6,000 drivers conducted by the National Highway Traffic Safety Administration, the majority of motorists consider unsafe driving by others a significant threat to their personal safety. A third of them thought that drivers in their area were behaving more aggressively than a year ago. Reasons cited were traveling at unsafe speeds, weaving in and out of traffic, tailgating, being inattentive, and making unsafe lane changes.[2] Obviously a few of us are not good drivers!

In this and the next three chapters that follow, we present a totally new way of thinking about driving. We discuss reasons to be concerned about making a trip in the first place and, once on the road, we show how important it is to be proactive in a systematic way—anticipating so that we can react sooner and easily, quickly, and effectively. Our goal is to drive in a seamless and predictable manner.

Introduction to Proactive Driving

A Car Is a Car Is a Car

Law enforcement officers, lawyers and insurance agents love the word "vehicle." It sounds so official. But since this book is not about large trucks, I will use the word "car." In today's usage, the word "car" is the same as "auto" and includes sedans, coupes, compacts, sport utility vehicles, minivans, crossovers, hybrids, and even small pickup trucks.

The Official State Driver's Manual

This book assumes that you already are a licensed driver. Nevertheless, if you took your test some years ago, it would be extremely beneficial for you to scoot down to your local Department of Motor Vehicles and pick up the current copy of your state driver's manual. The publication is usually free and makes a great coffee table item. It has clear diagrams of vehicles interacting safely with each other as well as beautiful color pictures (usually of your state house, your current governor, and a whole host of traffic signs). Most importantly it contains an entire truckload of the latest and safest information on how to drive and avoid crashes. Many of these manuals may be downloaded as PDFs from your state Department of Motor Vehicles.

A Crash Is Not an Accident

Most of what we are used to calling motor vehicle "accidents" can actually be avoided; but a true accident cannot. The traffic safety community calls this a "crash." When you come upon the word "accident" in this book, ask yourself if it could have been avoided. If so, you may change the word to "crash."

The Manufacturers' Curse

The manufacturers have made our cars so comfortable and easy to drive that we are under the false impression that such ease allows us to talk on a cell phone, text, fiddle with an elaborate stereo system, type on our computers, follow our route on a visual navigation system, watch a video news display, or any number of other activities as we drive. When we do this, we are depending on the skills of our fellow drivers to avert a crash. In-car gadgets and dependence on other drivers are false gods that can betray us in an instant. We must ignore distractions and stay alert if we wish to drive safely.

A Just-in-Time Society

Today we use credit cards instead of savings to purchase big-ticket items. This is *just-in-time* financing. Manufacturers keep small inventories, counting on just-in-time deliveries of component parts. Drivers wait until an emergency develops before they put aside their cell phones, stop adjusting their radio dials, or turn from a discussion with their passenger. This is an unfortunate and potentially disastrous application of the just-in-time concept.

While they may think it will be just-in-time, it is actually just too late. They have missed the opportunity to avert a crash.

Just-in-time driving is incredibly illogical. My daughter found that out when she neglected to fill her gas tank and ran out of fuel at night on a lonely road. Most of us do fill our gas tanks before they are empty. And many of us do religiously take our car for scheduled maintenance. Yet, we can still be guilty of just-in-time driving once we are on the road.

Defensive Driving

Most drivers are familiar with the term *defensive driving*. Defensive Driving is a form of driver training that goes beyond mastery of the rules of the road and the basic mechanics of driving. Its aim is to reduce the risk of driving by anticipating dangerous situations despite adverse conditions or the mistakes of others. It is, in effect, the exact opposite of just-in-time driving. Defensive driving can be achieved through adherence to a variety of general rules as well as the practice of specific driving techniques.[3] Defensive driving has been taught for many decades and forms a sound basis for safe driving techniques.

Proactive Driving

This book will introduce you to *proactive driving*, a term that is popping up in driver education literature. My definition of proactive driving takes defensive driving one giant step further. It provides drivers with a proactive format for anticipating rather than reacting to driving crises. Both routine and emergency driving situations demand split-second decisions. When driving, the proactive driver uses a series of repetitive thought processes to stay constantly alert, thereby reducing the time needed to make these critical decisions. The proactive driver also plans carefully before driving, aiming to eliminate or avoid dangerous situations that lead to a crash. This is just as important because the die can be cast for a mishap the instant that the driver starts their vehicle and, once on the highway, even the best driver can do very little to avoid a serious accident. Many things might come to your mind, such as intoxication, bald tires, poor brakes, or icy roads.

The First Rule of Three: Scouting, Deciding, and Acting

The proactive driver is continually scouting the road ahead, deciding on the best driving response and acting upon that decision. This is the first and most important of several rules of three that we will examine in this book.

Scouting

Proactive drivers spend much more time than other drivers looking over the road ahead, down side roads, in their rearview mirrors, and at other items that could affect them. Doing this periodically keeps them alert and involved. At the same time, they maintain their primary focus on vehicles and road conditions in their immediate proximity. They will often glance ahead twice within seconds to help detect moving items that are hard to see such as motorcycles or pedestrians. Scouting "ahead" is actually a misnomer. You should be glancing in as many directions as possible. But only glance briefly—less than a second—unless you see something important. Here are some of the things you should be watching for:

- The condition and speed of the vehicles in front of you
- The condition of the road
- Oncoming cars on both the main road and side roads
- Shifting or falling loads on trucks in front of you
- People, animals, tree limbs, or other obstacles in the road
- A car or truck coming up on you from the rear at a reckless speed
- Wind speed and direction (from flags, chimney smoke)
- Storm clouds on the horizon

Deciding

Once something unexpected is identified, the proactive driver analyzes it to determine if a dangerous situation is developing. For example, let's say that you see a car approaching on a side street. As it nears the main highway, it fails to slow. Will it ignore the stop sign and shoot out onto the highway in front of you? Obviously, you have to decide what might happen and what to do about it to avoid a crash. The information that follows throughout the book will assist you in honing your decision-making.

Acting

In this example, your action should be to slow down until the approaching vehicle halts at the stop sign. By detecting the vehicle early on, you can avoid emergency braking, a last minute swerve into the oncoming lane, or even a crash if the other vehicle does not stop.

It's very important to remember that this process should repeat itself continuously as you move along. Just as soon as you see the other vehicle slowing, you will sweep your gaze across the horizon again to see what else might be coming up. In fact, if the other vehicle had not stopped, you might have looked ahead to see if the oncoming lane was clear, or to the side to see if you could use the shoulder to go behind the vehicle as it shoots across the intersection. Once the situation is resolved, you will again focus primarily on the traffic immediately in front of you.

When planning a trip, the proactive driver will strive to reduce the number of these decisions. For example, he might use a freeway whenever possible instead of a local road to eliminate the threat from oncoming drivers and eliminate the hazards caused by vehicles entering from side streets.

Time and Space

Senior drivers have difficulties with depth perception. This means that it is hard for them to judge how far away an approaching car is. Such judgment is essential in making a left turn against traffic and the elderly have a disproportionately high frequency of accidents during this move.[4] However, all driving depends on this concept, which deals with time and space.

While you may be concerned about what will happen to your car where it is at this instant, you've already made the decision that put your vehicle there. Instead, you should be even more focused on the road ahead. What you want to do is make a decision now that avoids your car from entering a space down the road that is occupied by another vehicle when you get there. If it is, *whamo*! You have a crash.

For example, you're zipping down the interstate at 70 miles per hour. Did you know that your car will be 513 feet down the road in just 5 seconds? That's over 1½ soccer fields or 30 car lengths away. That also just happens to be slightly less than the distance that you will need to bring your vehicle to a halt at that speed. The following table gives you the distance that you travel in two seconds and five seconds at various speeds:

Speed	Distance Traveled in 2 Seconds	Distance Traveled in 5 Seconds
10 mph	29 ft.	73 ft.
20	59	147
30	88	220
40	117	293
50	147	367
60	176	440
70	205	513

Table 1: Distance traveled in 2 seconds and 5 seconds at different speeds.

No wonder the proactive driver looks ahead. Try to visualize these two distances the next time that you drive, and plan ahead based on where your car will be, not where it is now. This should make clear the need for looking ahead as far as possible when you drive. And look again at the first column. It will help you to know what the interval should be between you and the car ahead. For safety purposes, experts consider two seconds to be the absolute minimum time for this gap.

Future Chapters

Chapter 2 follows up this chapter with more rules of three. It concludes with a ten-point checklist for becoming a proactive driver. Chapter 3 suggests that reading other drivers is an important part of being proactive. Distracted drivers, the opposite of proactive drivers, are discussed in Chapter 4. Chapter 5 provides critical information that you should know about cars and highways. Chapter 6 then talks about situations that you may meet once you are on the road. Chapters 7 and 8 are special chapters on driving in winter and dealing with emergencies, respectively. Chapters 9 and 10 review critical safety issues relating to teenage and senior drivers. The last two chapters highlight key national issues and offer brief conclusions regarding the overall driving experience.

Use the table of contents to help you find the items that interest you. As you read, you will see how the proactive technique of scouting, deciding, and acting can be applied to a whole host of driving situations. Do not get discouraged just because so many of these topics offer the potential for a crash. Knowing of this potential actually makes driving much safer for you.

CHAPTER 2 – THE PROACTIVE DRIVER

As you have probably already discovered, driving is a rather complex activity. This chapter presents more rules of three that form the basis for driving in a systematic fashion. These include dividing the braking process into its three major components, maintaining a safe distance behind other vehicles, staying off the road when it's appropriate, and using other senses as well as eyesight. As we do this, the necessity of leaving enough time for our trip and being courteous to other drivers becomes clear. With this information we can present ten steps for becoming a proactive driver.

The Second Rule of Three: Minimize Perception, Reaction, and Braking Time

Stopping a car in an emergency occurs in a three-step sequence: perceiving, reacting, and braking. Were you ever in an old-fashioned driver education car that demonstrated this sequence? They used to have three pistols temporarily bolted to the front bumper. The pistols pointed at the ground. You, the student, were instructed to hit the brakes when you heard a shot. The instructor then told you to take the car up to 30 miles per hour. Bang! The instructor fired the first gun. You hit the brakes hard. Your three classmates in the back seat flew onto the floor (not really). The second gun went off. Yeah, it was triggered by your foot hitting the brake.

The car stopped. The instructor fired the third gun. You and your classmates piled out of the vehicle and stared in wonder at the three powder marks on the pavement. At 30 miles per hour, the car had traveled a total of 88 feet. Of that, you had already traveled 33 feet between the time that you heard the first shot and the time that your foot hit the brake pedal. In this calculation it took you 3/4 of a second to hit the brake, including about 1/4 of a second to move your foot from the accelerator to the brake and the rest to depress the pedal. Hitting the pedal is what fired the second gun.

Now for the second rule of three: Minimize your perception time to stop quickly in an emergency. Perception time is the only one of the three components (perception, reacting, braking) that you can substantially reduce by being alert. You were young and ready for the gun in the Driver Ed car so your reaction time was about as fast as possible. According to research, your total reaction time could have doubled to as much as 1 ½ seconds if you had been inattentive.[1]

So let's say you didn't know that first shot was coming. How much farther would you have traveled before you hit the brakes? Another 33 feet could result in a crash. At 70 miles per hour, a slow reaction time (1 ½ seconds) would result in traveling 154 feet before you applied your brakes. That is another half a soccer field or 10 car lengths! The table below gives the distances that it takes to stop at other speeds if we assume the optimistic reaction time of three-quarters of a second. The braking distances shown are for the most ideal of conditions: dry, level pavement:[2]

Speed	20mph	30mph	40mph	50mph	60mph	70mph
Distance traveled between stimulus & braking	22 ft.	33 ft.	44 ft.	55 ft	66 ft.	77 ft.
Distance traveled while braking	25 ft.	55 ft.	105 ft.	188 ft.	300 ft.	455 ft.
Total distance in feet	47 ft.	88 ft.	149 ft.	243 ft.	366 ft.	532 ft.
Total distance in car lengths	3	6	9	15	23	33

Table 2: Braking distances at different speeds

The Third Rule of Three: Maintain a Three-Second Gap

The third rule of three has to do with how we make sure that we are always ready for an emergency. While we drive, we alternate our focus between the road five seconds or more ahead and the traffic immediately in front of us. We constantly scout out our route in order to anticipate developing situations. This is the core of proactive driving. As in defensive driving, we still spend most of our time assessing the traffic situation immediately in front of us and taking appropriate action. But, by looking ahead frequently to the spot that we'll reach in five seconds, we are better able to see an emergency situation developing.

We mentioned at the end of the last chapter that two seconds is the absolute minimum gap of time between our car and the vehicle ahead. The most desirable gap is actually four seconds. However, it is extremely difficult to maintain this gap if other drivers have the opportunity to pass you, as they will see the gap between you and the car ahead as an ample space for them to occupy. Until more drivers are willing to honor a longer gap, you should at least aim for a three-second spacing between your vehicle and the one ahead, our next rule of three. The three-second gap gives just enough time to react and brake safely in an emergency.

Unfortunately, the two-second gap may be thrust upon us in heavier traffic. Going to the two-second gap is often the only way to protect yourself from someone cutting in front of you and reducing a three-second gap to 1–1 ½ seconds, a very unsafe condition that can lead quickly to a rear-end crash.

The Fourth Rule of Three: See, Hear, and Feel

A *huge* problem today is our foolish assumption that we need only our eyesight to drive. We really need our ears and our sense of feeling as well. What do we need our ears for? The most important use is for that blind spot in the driver's side mirror. We may glance briefly to our left side and miss seeing an overtaking car that is almost alongside of us. Then, when we pull out to change lanes, *blam*! Being able to detect the sound of that passing car is the real reason that we turn off our radio and cell phone. And there are plenty of other reasons, including reacting quickly to an ambulance siren or blaring horn.

How about our sense of feeling? We get it best if we have both hands on the wheel. Say you are driving in a downpour and your car is about to hydroplane. You will need both your ears (to hear the water under your tires) and your sense of feeling (to detect the first hint that you're losing traction). In winter, you also need to feel the slipperiness or hear the crunch of your tires on snow (see Chapter 7 on winter driving).

The Fifth Rule of Three: Three Seconds of Inattention Kills

If you do not look at the road for one second, you are quite likely to drift into the opposing lane or the ditch. Three seconds of inattention will likely result in a crash. This is why texting while driving and falling asleep at the wheel are two examples of incredibly dangerous driving.

The Sixth Rule of Three: Know When to Stay Home

The sixth rule of three has to do with when not to drive. If you are intoxicated or if the roads are sheer ice, that's reason enough for not getting behind the wheel. The proactive driver thinks carefully about this before starting the car. Accidents often happen due to a combination of factors. For instance, imagine venturing out at night into a raging snowstorm with a car that has bald tires. This or any other combination of three separate circumstances including being in a hurry, tired, distracted, or under the influence of alcohol, drugs, or medications, even in small amounts, is a formula for disaster. To make this point, we'll first make a few lists. These include:

- Driver condition
    - Tired
    - Poor eyesight
    - Over age 75
    - Controlling misbehaving children or pets
    - Faced with a personal crisis, upset emotionally
    - Rushing to meet a deadline
    - Under the influence of alcohol, drugs, or prescribed medications

- Auto condition
    - Bald tires
    - Faulty brakes
    - Worn wiper blades
    - Burned-out headlight
    - Alignment problems
    - Overloaded vehicle

- Road conditions
    - Bumper-to-bumper traffic
    - Solar glare (driving into the sun)
    - Heavy rain or flooding
    - High winds
    - Fog or darkness

As you read these, you'll probably think of a dozen or more items to add. If you can circle three things on these lists, you may be greatly increasing the chances of having a crash. And, it is not necessarily going to be caused by an item that you've circled, but by a fourth that you have overlooked or for which you did not plan.

For example, let's say that you're in a hurry to get to Aunt Suzie's and the kids are fighting in the back seat. You're traveling on a wet freeway in heavy traffic and the tread on your tires is not the best. The temperature rapidly drops, the pavement freezes, and someone ahead of you skids. You are suddenly involved in a chain-reaction crash involving two dozen vehicles. It is easy to miss a weather report if you are in a hurry. It's easy to travel too closely to the vehicle in front if you are turning in your seat to quell World War III. Whatever the items you've circled, be aware that if you circle three, you are putting yourself in much greater jeopardy if you travel. Stay home!

The Seventh and Final Rule of Three: Three Tickets? You're Gone

Even the Motor Vehicle Bureau folks have a rule of three: If you get three speeding tickets within a given length of time (typically three years), you lose your license! Of course, the lawyers have gotten their hands on this one, so it often comes with all sorts of caveats that vary from state to state. Don't be fooled. Your license is in jeopardy as soon as you get your first speeding ticket. That is because your second ticket has to be your last or your license is gone. Think about it!

Highlights Rather Than Illustrations
The main focus of this book is to show you how you can use the proactive driving techniques that we just described to improve your driving knowledge and skills. Towards this end the text includes many significant and helpful facts that readers may not know. However, we omit detailed illustrations due to space limitations. Those interested in seeing illustrations can find them in the publications listed in Appendix 2.

Timing
Allow plenty of time for your trip. This will greatly reduce your anxiety on the road. With a little extra time, proactive drivers can rearrange their lives to greatly reduce the risk of crashes. For example, if you leave extra time, you can take a longer but safer route if one is available. At the risk of sounding repetitive, another important timing skill is knowing when to say "No" to travel when it is unsafe. Know when it's time to stay put!

Be Courteous
Since a lack of courtesy is the number one complaint of today's drivers, let's finish up with how easy it is for the proactive driver to be a courteous driver as well. A driver is usually judged to be discourteous because of continuously contesting the space available on the road. When the discourteous driver/fighter achieves a tie, he loses. His car crashes into another vehicle. Meanwhile our proactive driver spends much of her time planning ways to avoid hitting other vehicles. A courteous or proactive driver has scouted ahead, recognized the possibility of a crash, and taken positive action to avoid it. Obviously, the courteous driver is a safe driver. Can we infer that the discourteous driver is not? It should be easy for you to decide. Please see the section on courtesy in Chapter 6 for some more ideas.

Our Goal: Seamless Driving

You may be a licensed driver and have already taken to the road. We are assuming that you are familiar with traffic laws and possess the basic skills to maneuver your car effectively. For you as a driver, this means constant awareness and anticipation. To other drivers, it means your vehicle moves seamlessly through traffic. You fit smoothly into the traffic stream and other drivers can predict your actions. You may check yourself. Do you pass as many vehicles as have passed you? Unfortunately, this may mean exceeding the speed limit by a few miles per hour. Seamless driving will benefit you too. How? It will minimize the difference in speed between your car and the other vehicles, thereby reducing the likelihood of a crash.

The Proactive Driver: A Summary

Note that we do not use any magical formulas, but we are, first and foremost, alert. We are constantly and systematically checking and evaluating the road and cars around us.

Before leaving home, make sure it is safe to make the trip: Use the rules of three for driver, auto, road, and traffic conditions to decide if you should make the trip.

Be mindful of where your car will be: Once underway, take actions as a driver that assure that the space ahead of you will be unoccupied by another car by the time you get there.

Follow the scouting, deciding, and acting steps described in Chapter 1: In short, constantly scout ahead, as well as to the side and rear. Pay especially close attention to all areas of the road in front of you.

Be alert: Perceiving an emergency and reacting quickly can save your life.

Keep a safe distance between you and the vehicle in front of you: Four seconds is ideal, three seconds is acceptable, and two seconds is the absolute minimum.

Use all three of your important senses: Your sense of hearing and your feel for the wheel are just as necessary as your eyesight in alerting you to danger.

Be a courteous driver: Don't contest highway space with other motorists; let them have it. And, if you can, perform at least one act of kindness towards another driver each time that you get behind the wheel.

Be a predictable driver: Enter, travel in, and leave traffic flows seamlessly. And always use your turn signals, brake lights, or headlights to signal your intentions.

Learn to read the behavior of other drivers: Become skilled in reading the actions of the drivers in front of you. It will keep you alert and help you anticipate their next move.

Rehearse your reactions to emergencies in advance: You will read about ways to deal with a wide variety of emergency situations in Chapters 6, 7, and 8. Keep these in mind each time that you drive, visualize the possibility of them happening in front of you, and rehearse your reaction.

CHAPTER 3 – LEARNING TO READ OTHER DRIVERS

ON CURVES AHEAD
REMEMBER, SONNY
THAT RABBIT'S FOOT
DIDN'T SAVE THE BUNNY

Burma-Shave

In Chapters 1 and 2 we highlighted the importance of 1) looking ahead to where your car will be; and 2) minimizing the distractions that are possible from, for example, phoning or texting while behind the wheel. Now it's time to refocus on the area immediately around you. Being aware of drivers, cyclists, and pedestrians nearby and reading their actions can be just as important for avoiding dangerous situations.

We've already talked about how you might identify a driver in front of you who is phoning or texting. You also can predict the behavior of other drivers in front of you. Then, you can better estimate the path of their vehicle, thereby avoiding a possible crash. In the cases of criminal behavior, early detection might save your life. Reading other drivers also is an extremely excellent way for you to stay alert and involved as you drive.

Consider Letting Tailgaters Pass You

We get quite nervous when we see someone coming up from behind us at high speed. Tailgaters are really apprentice road ragers. They are annoyed because you are not going faster, even if it means exceeding the speed limit. Seeing a rapidly approaching tailgater in our rearview mirror is sure to divert our attention from the road ahead. If this happens, a proactive driver will signal, pull over if there is a safe place to do so, and let the tailgater pass. Otherwise, that rear-end collision is a distinct possibility. Why? Very simply, if you suddenly have to brake, the tailgater will run into you. Because the gap between your two cars is less than two seconds, they cannot react in time to avoid a crash. The fact that your gas tank is in the back of your car can make this type of collision very dangerous.

Some recommend that you tap your brakes without slowing to communicate to the car behind that it is too close. However, this *is not* a good idea if that person continues to aggressively tailgate you. If you continue to tap your brakes frequently, the tailgater may ram you when you have to use the brakes for real. Sometimes it may just be someone in a hurry and letting them pass you as soon as possible solves the problem.

Move Out of the Way of Reckless Drivers

Reckless drivers, road ragers, and those driving while impaired are extremely dangerous because their actions are unpredictable. For varying reasons, they may suddenly and unexpectedly attempt to occupy the space where your vehicle is, causing a serious crash. Quite often, you don't see the reckless driver in time to take evasive action. If you look ahead of you often or check your rearview mirror frequently, you increase your chances of spotting them. Once spotted, you may have only seconds to act. Unfortunately, it is difficult to deal rationally with their irrationality. You probably should not make any sudden moves, as the space that you move to may be the one that they want to be in. One strategy is to slowly decrease your speed and move to the side of the road. If one roars up alongside you and brakes for a vehicle in front of them, it is likely that they want to cut over into your lane. Slow down and give them room. And be aware that sometimes there may be two or three vehicles chasing one another.

Give Road Ragers All the Room You Can

Road rage is a relatively recent development (see section in Chapter 6 on "Road Rage"). While it can take many forms, it is basically an irrational reaction to your driving, one in which the rager may attempt to ram you with their vehicle, or cut you off and try to fight you, or even shoot you. Give a wide berth and make every effort to get out of the rager's way safely. In more mild cases, slowing down and letting the rager speed off works. If the driver persists, drive your car to a police station or a well-lit place with lots of people. Never attempt to retaliate or carry on the argument. If possible, get a license plate number or description of the vehicle or driver. Call 911 and report it and your location to the police. Cell phones are handy for this.

Stalkers

Stalkers are of concern at any time of day, but can be particularly unnerving at night. If you think you are being followed and you have a phone with you, use a hands-free device to call 911 immediately. If possible, give the operator the license plate number of the suspected stalker and a description of the driver or vehicle. Keep traveling as you do this and follow the recommendations of the operator. Lock your doors and drive towards a police station if one is nearby. If you are far from the police or you don't have a phone, drive to a populated, well-lit place like a store. When you arrive, lean on the horn to get the attention of other people and tell them what's going on. Ask someone to call 911.

Impaired Drivers

Impaired drivers are particularly oblivious to other cars, traffic signals, or pavement markings. Some drunk drivers, particularly younger ones, will speed. Older ones may drive very slowly. Often, the substance-impaired driver will weave back and forth. It may not be rapid weaving, but one in which they seem to suddenly notice that they are wandering to one side and will then steer the other way. Since they are irrational, it is best to stay as far away as possible. If you must pass them, wait until they weave to the right and then do so quickly on the left. Get their plate number and vehicle description, note your location, and call the police.

Teenagers

Teens often slow down and speed up or move from side to side in the traffic lane. One of the more common characteristics of these inexperienced drivers is a lack of attention. This manifests itself in unpredictable speed changes as they suddenly become aware that they are slowing down.

Other Erratic Drivers

Examples of other erratic drivers can include a car full of debating political fanatics, or even a driver who frequently turns to talk to the person in the passenger seat. The best thing to do is slow down and create a large space between your vehicle and the erratic driver until it is safe to pass. And if you see a crash situation developing in front of you, do not assume that the inexperienced or inattentive driver ahead of you also sees it.

One Pedal Pressure Fits All

Seniors often drive slowly to compensate for their age-affected eyesight and reaction time. Some do not vary their pressure on the gas pedal. Thus they are "gravity drivers": those whose cars slow down on the uphills and speed up on the downhills. This is frustrating for other drivers because these drivers will speed up just as you attempt to pass. If you are a senior driver, you should guard against developing this driving habit. Check your rear-view mirror and slow down so other vehicles can pass you.

If you're stuck behind a gravity driver, try to find a safe spot to do a "flying pass," whereby you first slow down to increase the gap between your vehicles as you start up the hill, and then increase your speed before the downhill begins. You can then pull out and pass before the gravity driver attains terminal velocity. Of course, only pass if you can see that the road ahead is clear, and that you can do so without exceeding the speed limit.

The Unduly Cautious

This driver will slow for overhanging trees, buildings close to the highway and other perceived "obstacles" that are not close enough to the roadway to constitute a hazard.

One Speed Fits All

It is an unaware motorist who drives at a constant speed. "One speed fits all" means it is usually an agonizing slow speed for interstates and an illegally fast speed through school zones. These motorists often are driving at speeds that differ considerably from the rest of the traffic. This can make them very dangerous.

Driving Without Lights and Other Maladies

Most of us drive with our lights on at all times. Be particularly wary of a driver who has the headlights off at dusk or at night. That driver will be difficult to see and may be impaired. A variation is the "Padiddle." This is a car with only one headlight. You should be extra careful when driving near these since the driver who is unaware of a burned out headlight may be unaware of other drivers. Or the unaware driver may be operating a car that is badly dented or out of alignment. An out-of-alignment car is much more likely to fishtail or even roll over if its driver slams on the brakes.

Smoking Exhaust Pipe

Clear, visible smoke from the tailpipe of the car in front of you indicates that it has just started on its trip. It is a time when the car's driver may not be totally attentive. Of course a car with black smoke pouring from its exhaust system also may suggest that an inattentive driver is behind the wheel.

License Plates and Stickers

License plates are a good source of information. Some states even identify the county of residence on their plates. And vanity plates may give you an insight into the personality of the motorist in front of you. Stickers can give you their political affiliation or their pet project. I don't know that the information is always useful, but it can be very entertaining. My favorite bumper sticker reads "Stop Continental Drift."

Make, Model, Age, and Condition

Remember, our objective here is to learn what other drivers might do. Sometimes we can even try to predict their behavior based on the make, model, age, or condition of the vehicle. Some researchers in Great Britain have even attempted to link driver personalities to car color. Their survey was based on 130,000 insurance claims. It started with the most dangerous colors.[1] But it may only apply to new cars, and I am sure that you know that police often use black cars and, occasionally, white cars but very infrequently other colors.

- Driving a black car suggests an aggressive personality.
- Silver cars indicate someone who is cool, calm, and slightly aloof.
- Green cars are often the choice of people with hysterical tendencies.
- Yellow cars signify someone who is idealistic and novelty loving.
- Blue cars are chosen by more introspective and cautious drivers.
- Grey cars represent those who are calm, sober, and dedicated to their work.
- Red cars denote people full of zest and energy and who think and move quickly.
- Pink cars are chosen by gentle, loving, and affectionate drivers.

- White cars represent status-seeking extroverts.
- Cream-color cars denote self-contained and controlled drivers.

It is interesting to note that red cars are banned in Shanghai, China.

Use All the Information Available

Car watching can tell you about the nature of the trip as well as the driver. Let's say you come upon a very old car with a smoking tailpipe. You might assume that the car has just started its trip. You could also guess that an older car is less likely to be taken on a long trip. Put these two together and you will be watching for the car to turn off the road soon.

An out-of-state plate may mean that the driver is unfamiliar with the local area. A poorly maintained car suggests a careless driver and probably a short trip. Once you acquire some skill at this, you will astound yourself at your ability to predict the moves of the car ahead. But remember, drive on the basis of what is happening, not what you think might happen.

Driveways, Sidewalks, and Lawns

Watch the activity along the side of the roadway as well. You may be passing cyclists. In residential areas, cars may be backing out of driveways into your lane. Or, children or pets playing on the sidewalk may dart into the road in pursuit of a ball. Be sure to slow down if you see these potential hazards developing.

One autumn afternoon, I was driving on a desolate, wooded road that twisted and turned. It had just rained and newly fallen leaves had made the pavement extremely slippery. Before one particularly sharp turn, I noticed a teen walking up a driveway. I immediately slowed down. Sure enough, as I rounded the corner there was a school bus stopped in front of me. If I hadn't figured out why that teen was walking up the drive at that time of day, I would have skidded into the back of that bus!

Driving as an Educational Tool

Driver observation skills can be taught to children at a very young age. It is one way of letting children know that driving is not "boring, boring, boring." Parents could start with very simple games such as counting convertibles, trucks, school buses, dogs, horses, etc. More advanced games available for young riders include car bingo. In this game the first person to see an object depicted on their bingo card checks it off. You can buy "car bingo" as a packaged game, or make your own cards together after talking about what you're likely to see. The winner is the first person to check off all the items in a row, column, or diagonal line on the game card. As they become older they could look for specific types of homes, trees, field crops, or even the geological features that determine the route that a highway takes. If they look closely, they will see many items that were introduced to them in their science classes.

This is not just a good way for the young to develop an awareness and enjoyment of driving; when they become adults, learning to observe the route they take can provide them with useful information such as a quicker route in case of a traffic delay or even the location of a store that they would like to visit.

And there are often surprise benefits to this type of awareness. After searching for several years during my drives in the country I finally spotted an architectural example of what the missing porch on my farmhouse may have looked like. I photographed the porch and was able to replicate it on the front of my house.

CHAPTER 4 – THE DISTRACTED DRIVER

Distracted driving is the exact opposite of proactive driving. Why? Because distractions such as texting or cell phone conversations steal your attention away from the road ahead. In fact, *distraction, delay,* and *disaster* are the exact three words that driving instructors use to identify the chain of events that end in a crash.

The National Safety Council estimates that drivers talking on cell phones cause 1.4 million crashes a year and driving while texting is responsible for at least two hundred thousand additional crashes.[1] The Federal Department of Transportation estimates that six thousand people were killed and another five hundred thousand injured in these crashes.[2] It is ample evidence that dialing your phone, reading a text message or glancing at a map display on your dashboard does distract you for that split second of attention that can result in a crash. USDOT is not the only one who recognizes this problem. On September 19, 2013, AT&T initiated a nationwide campaign entitled "It Can Wait." Signs repeating the slogan are appearing at pull-outs on interstate highways in New York State. Below the slogan are the words, "3 Text Violations—Lose License."

The common theme in distracted driving is temporarily taking your eyes off the road. Many distractions, and especially texting, actually divert your attention from the road for several seconds. This greatly increases the likelihood of a crash. But even if you don't take your eyes off the road, your conversation on a cell phone focuses a significant portion of your mind on the call, taking your full concentration away from the road in front of you. What often happens is that the driver omits the "Scouting" portion of proactive driving first described in Chapter 1. Their driving focus tends to narrow and zero in on the road immediately in front of their car. This can prevent them from seeing a serious situation developing down the road or to their side.

Distracted drivers can be identified in various ways. Some will weave slowly from side to side and then jerk their car back when they start to come into the adjoining lane. Others will slow down, often suddenly, for no apparent reason. Or they will abruptly slow and pull off the road, again for no apparent reason. This last action is, of course, the most desirable one if they use their blinkers and slow gradually.

Many of us can cite examples of narrowly avoided crashes caused by distracted drivers. My most recent incident occurred while traveling at 65 miles per hour in the right lane on I-495 outside of Boston. An SUV shot down an entrance ramp at over 70 miles per hour and entered my lane without pause. As I hit the brakes to avoid a crash, I saw the driver with a cell phone pressed to his left ear and his eyes staring vacantly ahead. His other hand had to be holding the steering wheel in a death grip to keep the vehicle in the center of the curving ramp. His cell phone and his steering wheel occupied all his attention and actually made it impossible for him to look to his left and see that the lane he was entering was already occupied!

Talking on a Cell Phone

The use of cell phones while driving is skyrocketing. This is dangerous for two reasons. The first is that you will be so deep into a conversation that you will not notice a developing accident situation. The second is that you have taken your sense of hearing out of your driving response ability. Quite often, an impending crash is preceded by sounds such as a horn or squealing brakes. If you can't hear these, how can you possibly take corrective action?

If you are behind the wheel and are sending or receiving a call on your cell phone, ask yourself if this call is important enough to risk your life. It is not the time or place to simply pass the time of day. A second question is whether this call is an emergency or requires a well-thought-out response. If so, pull over, develop your response, and call back.

Cell phone users often feel safe because they are still watching the road ahead as they converse. But all that they really are watching is a small area of the road directly in front of their car.[3] Our advice? Make all your calls before you leave the house. Twenty-six states currently ban the use of hand-held instruments while driving.[4]

Being a Crash Enabler

Have you ever called or texted someone when you knew they were in their car driving somewhere? Shame on you. You are knowingly creating a potential crash situation. Here are two examples of problems that callers created:

First, my friend became instantly distracted from driving. Thinking it may be an emergency, he was suddenly in a rush to answer his cell phone before it stopped ringing. He reached in his pocket for the phone. But he couldn't get it out without twisting his body in the driver's seat and unbuckling his seat belt. Then he had to rebuckle his seat belt with one hand as he answered the phone with the other. Not only was he not watching the traffic, but at some point he actually had to take both hands off the steering wheel.

Second, my wife received a call while driving. As the phone rang her concentration shifted from the drivers around her to the quest for her phone. Her phone was in her purse at her feet. She immediately reached down with one hand and discovered that her purse was zipped shut. She braced one knee against the steering wheel and used both hands to unzip the purse. She then checked several compartments before she found her phone. If her bag had been on the passenger seat, she would have had to turn to her right to peek at the seat and then lean over, grab her purse, and unzip it. If this had happened there was a strong possibility that she would have unconsciously turned the steering wheel to the right and driven off the road.

So please don't call your friends or relatives if you know they are driving. And if you do reach someone who is driving, ask the driver to pull over and call you back. Even better, tell them that you will hang up after two rings as a signal for them to pull over and call you back. If someone calls while you are driving, wait to answer or check messages until you come to a stop. And if you're the passenger and the driver starts using their phone, ask them to please pull over to the side of the road.

Of course, for those who can afford them, there are a number of sophisticated assists such as a dashboard-mounted phone and hands-free devices that eliminate these mad scrambles. But sophisticated assists notwithstanding, the driver will still be distracted by the initial ringing of the device as well as by the conversation that follows. It will be especially distracting if it requires a decision on the part of the driver or informs him or her of a crisis.

Texting

Texting while driving is an entire order of magnitude more dangerous than talking on a cell phone. Texting drivers typically take their eyes off the road for as much as five seconds.[5] As pointed out in Chapter 2, focusing your eyes on your texting device for more than three seconds is extremely dangerous. You can also lose your feel for steering as you press those little keys. And, you are likely to take your mind off driving while you compose a message. What happens? Texting drivers often slow their vehicles (inviting a rear-end collision) or wander into an oncoming lane or the ditch. When you finally do look up, it frequently is too late to avoid a crash. To address this problem, AT&T offers an application (app) that automatically responds to incoming texts, letting the sender know that you are driving.

Finally, are you willing to risk a long stint in prison? Thirty states have already passed laws banning texting and more will do so in the future. If you are in a crash, then police investigators will obtain your phone records. Neither judges nor juries are sympathetic when these records show beyond a doubt that you were texting at the time of the crash. At this point, texting can become reckless driving and, if there is a death, vehicular homicide. Both crimes will put you in prison.

More Legislation Likely

Crashes are increasing as more and more people talk on cell phones or text. Just as with drunk driving, public outcry is likely to demand that stricter and stricter laws be passed to curb these inconsiderate and dangerous activities. One of many possibilities is to require manufacturers of hand-held devices to embed in these instruments technology that tells the driver that he has a call but renders them inoperable while the car is in motion.

Talking to a Passenger

Distracted driving is not limited to cell phones and texting. Talking to passengers, searching for an object or quelling child wars in the back seat can be equally distracting. My son-in-law is a gesticulator. While driving, he will look you in the eye and gesticulate with *both* hands. This is very scary! Why? Because when you turn your head, two things can occur. The first is that you will not see someone or something that suddenly moves in front of your car. The second is that you will tend to pull the steering wheel in the direction that you turn, possibly driving off the road.

Reading a Paper, Applying Makeup, or Eating

Anything else that ties up one of your hands or requires you to look down while you drive is dangerous, again because it can cause you to miss an object in your path or steer out of your lane.

Listening to Music, Especially with Earphones

Listening to loud music also takes away your ability to react to sound. This distraction is termed "Noise in the Cabin." It includes a loud radio and noisy riders. Talking on a cell phone or listening with earphones (usually illegal) can also rob you of your hearing. As mentioned in Chapter 2, you most need your hearing when you are driving on a freeway. On that type of road, one of your most dangerous acts will be pulling into the passing lane. There is a blind spot on your driver side mirror. This means that you can miss seeing a car that has pulled beside you. If so, you will collide with it as you move to your left. Many a time, I have been saved from this because I heard the vehicle coming up alongside me.

Rubbernecking

The term "rubbernecking" means turning your head to the side to see an accident or some other intriguing distraction along the side of the road. As you turn your head, you may inadvertently turn your steering wheel in the same direction and go off the highway. Or, you may crash into someone in front of you when they hit their brakes to avoid rear-ending the rubbernecker in front of them.

Breakdowns along the side of the road or in the opposite lane are not the only cause of rubbernecking fender benders. Some years ago, a huge, changeable-message billboard was erected on a curve leading to a busy intersection. Drivers simply could not read the sign, turn their car, and stop simultaneously. When the sign was removed, the rash of rear-end crashes at the intersection disappeared.

Reaching for a Falling Object

My aunt had a head-on crash in her brand new SUV when she reached over to right a fallen flower pot on the seat next to her. She was in the hospital for a month. She also totaled the car and lost her driver's license. Never reach or grab for anything. This includes your cell phone, papers, water bottles, or food.

Controlling Animals in the Car

See the section in Chapter 6 entitled "Animals in the Car."

Swatting at Insects

A bee in the car is the ultimate test of self-control. No matter what it's doing, pull to the side of the road and stop. Only then get rid of the bee. It may even be a good idea to keep the front windows rolled up. Bees have stung me in the arm when they were blown into the car at freeway speeds. Also pull over before trying to catch those buzzing flies that are always just out of reach.

Depending on Other Drivers

In all its forms, distracted driving is the newest and most dangerous form of just-in-time driving discussed in Chapter 1. You are, in effect, depending on other drivers to get out of your way if you cross the centerline and invade their lane. One can easily imagine that distracted driving crashes will increase exponentially as the percentage of drivers available to take action to avoid just-in-time drivers decreases.

Depending on Driving Assists

Many auto manufacturers now offer driver assists. Two common types are alarms that sound if you come too close to another vehicle and automated braking if you do not respond to the alarm. There is a very real risk that a distracted driver will use these assists on a regular basis and neglect looking ahead to detect and prevent crash situations. But sudden braking of their car can get them rear-ended. A better approach is to rely on these assists only for those very rare moments when you miss seeing that the car in front of you is slowing.

PART II
NUTS AND BOLTS

CHAPTER 5 – THINGS TO KNOW BEFORE YOU GO

DON'T LOSE
YOUR HEAD
TO GAIN A MINUTE
YOU NEED YOUR HEAD
YOUR BRAINS ARE IN IT

Burma-Shave

Attitude

You should never get behind the wheel if you are in a hurry or distracted by emotional issues. All attention must be directed toward your driving. You are about to take up to two tons of steel onto a highway and travel among other hunks of steel at speeds of 60 to 70 miles per hour. Distractions at these speeds can be deadly. If it is impossible not to be distracted, then you must assign yourself one of the three points that we suggested will cause you to abort your trip and stay home (see Chapter 2).

And speaking of distractions, once in the car forget about petting that dog in your lap, listening to loud music, turning to converse with friends, fiddling with the buttons or dials, using a cell phone, or texting. Instead, focus on the route that you are taking so that you can arrive safely at your destination (see Chapter 4, "The Distracted Driver").

Another way to focus on your driving is to do a favor for another driver each time that you hit the road. The other day I was passing a tractor-trailer when I saw a speeder behind me trying to insert his vehicle in my tailpipe. The trucker blinked his lights as soon as it was safe for me to pull back in and let the speeder pass. I was appreciative because it was a courtesy that he was not required to make. In fact, because of liability issues, he had probably been instructed by his employer to never dim his lights.

Are you one of those aggressive drivers who give other motorists the finger? For you, taping your fingers together with duct tape before driving may be considered a courtesy. (See the section in this chapter on "Courtesy," and Chapter 3, "Learning to Read Other Drivers.")

Finally, do not surprise the other drivers. Do what is expected and signal your intentions when possible. In the end, you will recall that you want to achieve a seamless drive where you fit into the traffic flow without disruption.

Before You Drive

Have you cleaned out your car recently? If so, you were probably amazed at all the "stuff" that you found. Part of being a proactive driver is to equip your vehicle with items that you need when you leave the house. You require some of these like the car keys, your driver's license, and money for gas for every trip. Other items you will need only occasionally but you will kick yourself mightily if you forget them. Here is a list of twenty important items. Another nine will be helpful if you plan to change a tire yourself. However, that plan will only work if you have already practiced a tire change in your driveway.

Basic Items

"Let's just get in the car and go." This is a plan. Not a good plan, but a plan. What you need is:

- Car keys
- Your driver's license
- Registration (copy)
- Insurance card and info
- Other Important Items

You also should have with you:

- A cell phone, prepaid phone card, or change for a telephone call
- Money for gas
- Telephone numbers of relatives to contact
- Pencil and paper
- Sunglasses, extra eyeglasses
- Road maps
- Flashlight with good batteries
- Window scraper
- Window cleaning cloth
- Any medications that you require

Items for Emergencies

You also should consider equipping your car with items for emergency situations. These include:

- First aid kit
- Tool kit
- Fire extinguisher

- Instant camera and film or phone with camera in case you have a crash
- Extra water
- Tow rope
- "Life Hammer" to cut your seat belt and break your side window after a roll-over

Tire Repairs

Consumer Reports suggests the following additional items for tire repairs:[1]

- Work gloves
- Flares or reflectors
- Blanket or rug to kneel on (or use floor mat)
- Tire pressure gauge
- Small 12-volt air compressor (these are not expensive)
- Pipe to slip over your tire wrench for extra leverage
- Plank to support the jack on soft ground
- Rags and hand cleaner
- Small container to hold lug nuts

Obviously, so much stuff is going to take a lot of trunk space. If you have hubcaps, you may want to omit the container for lug nuts. If you have a spare tire, you might eliminate the compressor. And if you have a cell phone and drive in an area with cell phone service, you could subscribe to a national road service such as the American Automobile Association (AAA). This would permit you to omit all but the flares or reflectors from your stash of tire stuff.

Another option for tire repair is the use of aerosol sealants and inflators.[2] If you have a flat tire, pump in the sealant and then pump up the tire with the inflator. However, be aware that the effectiveness of the sealant depends on the size and angle of the puncture. And, aerosol inflators will bring your tire up to only about 18 pounds per square inch or psi, but the pressure should be raised to the recommended levels (typically 40 psi) using the air compressor listed above. These puncture fixes are temporary and the tire should be repaired or replaced as soon as possible. The fixes should not be used for sidewall punctures. Instead, the tire should be replaced.

Winter Driving

Do you live in the north? If so, you will want to be prepared in case you are stranded in very cold weather. See Chapter 7, "Winter Driving," for some additional items that you will need.

Inform Others of Your Travel Plans

Besides having all the right stuff, be sure that someone knows where you're going and when you expect to return. If you're going to visit someone, it's polite to call and say, "We're leaving now" or, if it's a long trip, "we expect to arrive at your place in X minutes." If you are going on a longer trip, prepare written directions for yourself before you leave (See the section of this chapter entitled "Directions").

Do a Walk-Around

The very last thing to do before you get in your car is a quick walk-around. Check for children, animals, toys, or other obstructions in the drive. Also check for low tire pressure and oil or anti-freeze leaks. Then load your car from the curbside. As you load, make sure that there are no loose objects aboard that will become flying missiles if you stop suddenly.

If parked on the street, have your keys in your hand, look carefully for approaching traffic, and walk to the driver's door from the front of the car so that you can see oncoming traffic. Wait for a break in the traffic before opening the door, and open it only far enough and long enough to get into the vehicle.[3]

Before Starting the Engine

Once inside the car, it is time to lock the doors and adjust your seat and rearview mirrors. Clear the inside of your windows and check your head restraint if needed. Also adjust and fasten your seat belt.[4] Finally, start the car and test the brake pedal. Bon Voyage!

Capacity of Highways

Is the road you are headed for going to be at capacity? The capacity of a highway is defined as the number of cars per lane past a given point. Traffic engineers are extremely interested in whether a highway is at capacity during rush hours. If the road reaches capacity, backups will form and generate user delays and additional air pollution. We abhor delays. They are costly to us in terms of frustration, lost time, and missed appointments, not to mention the extra gas that our car consumes as it idles in a long queue.

Maximum Flow

It might help you to avoid these delays if you know at least a smidgen of highway capacity theory. As cars speed up, more pass a given point, hence, more capacity. All we need to do is get cars going about 120 miles per hour and we have much, much more capacity, right? Wrong! Maximum flow usually occurs somewhere between 35 and 45 miles per hour. How can that be? Obviously, at slower speeds, fewer cars pass that point. But what happens at higher speeds? At speeds exceeding 50 miles per hour, drivers intuitively increase the distance between their car and the vehicle ahead because of safety concerns.

When Backups Occur

How can this help you? Suppose you are zipping along the freeway at 65 miles per hour when traffic suddenly starts to slow. Perhaps this has happened before and you know of an alternate route. As your speed falls below 50 miles per hour you can consider diverting to that route. It will allow you to avoid the congestion that is about to happen. You see, once speeds drop below 35 to 45 miles per hour, backups will often occur. "Stop-and-go" driving conditions will prevail until the bottleneck clears.

Rubbernecking

If you are caught in a backup, you will be able to speed up once you are past the bottleneck. Backups often occur during crowded rush hours. But they also can be caused by a disabled vehicle, a traffic accident, a patrol car parked on the shoulder, or a very slow vehicle. You can even have a bottleneck on a freeway when there is an accident in the opposite lanes. This is called a "rubbernecking delay" because drivers on your side of the freeway are slowing to see what happened. Also see Chapter 4, "The Distracted Driver."

Congestion Pricing

Congestion pricing is a strategy for relieving congestion in the center of cities. Under congestion pricing, regulations require that drivers entering the downtown during rush hours must pay an additional fee for the privilege of occupying the streets at that time. Congestion pricing is currently used in Europe and Asia and is being actively considered for New York City; Boston, Massachusetts; and other U.S. cities. Details vary from proposal to proposal but it is likely to become more prevalent as congestion increases. An important benefit of the policy is a reduction in air pollution.

Dangerous and Safe Highways

There are over four million miles of highways in the United States. They include the following:[5]

Interstate highways	47,000 mi.
National highway system	117,000 mi.
State and local paved roads	2,466,000 mi.
Unpaved roads	1,402,000 mi.
Total	4,032,000 mi.

Table 3: Total miles of highways in the United States by highway type

The Most Dangerous Highways

Which of these roads should you try to avoid? The four-lane, undivided highway has over 4 crashes per million vehicle miles while a two-lane road produces 2.4 crashes per million vehicle miles. The reason that a four-lane, undivided highway is so much more dangerous is the huge number of driver decisions that the highway generates due to maneuvering and speed changes. Compared to a divided freeway, there is a virtually unlimited number of entrances and exits to businesses and homes. Intersections with other roads are at grade, which means that cars will be crossing the highway. Motorists are constantly changing lanes to turn left or right. They also are constantly adjusting their speeds as they enter or exit, or as they approach or leave traffic lights. If a car coming in the other direction loses control, it can easily come into your lane and cause a head-on crash.

Two-lane roads are safer than four-lane, undivided highways because the two-lane roads have less traffic and tend to have intersections and driveways spread out over greater distances. However, many two-lane highways also have design defects that are identified by warning signs. For example, there is a sharp but level curve near my previous home that becomes a hazard for speeding northbound motorists. A teenage girl lost control on that curve and ended up in a small but very deep pond just down the road. A farmer across the road looked out from his barn, saw the car sinking, dove into the pond, and pulled the girl out in the nick of time. So, if you are unfamiliar with the two-lane road that you are traveling, be cautious on the hills and curves! Also see the section entitled "Speed Limits" in Chapter 6.

The Safest Highways

Freeways typically experience only one crash per million vehicle miles. Not only is the number of driver decisions greatly reduced on a freeway, there is more time for drivers to act. Sight distances are greater, the two directions of traffic are separated, hills and curves are gentler, and the shoulders are wider for added safety. But not all freeways are equally safe. Typically, crash rates will increase as more vehicles use the route. For example, an interstate in a rural area may be safer than a freeway through the heart of a city such as Indianapolis. Also note that it is too expensive to build freeways in cities to the same standards as those in the country. Urban freeways tend to have more interchanges, narrower shoulders, steeper grades and sharper curves. That is why these roads normally have lower speed limits and higher accident rates.

That is not to say that the rural freeway is without its problems. In the early days of freeways, the designers decided that the more straight and level, the better. In western New York State, for example, the Thruway is extremely straight and level. But it is so boring that there is a high incidence of drivers falling asleep at the wheel. I-75 through South Georgia also is straight and level, but the high volume of traffic there is anything but boring.

Other interstates could not be located on level plains because these were already thickly settled. These so-called "hillside interstates" can be found halfway up the sides of the surrounding valleys. Such locations are subject to rock and mud slides unless the slopes have been cut back and safety fences installed to eliminate that problem. However, they still are prone to icing and fog and must be driven with this in mind. They also must dip and rise as they pass a side valley leading into the main valley, so slow moving vehicles may be encountered.

Three-Lane Highways

Three-lane highways are not in common use today because of the danger that two cars traveling in opposite directions will attempt to pass the car in front of them at the same time. To do so, they must both occupy the center lane. Obviously, a head-on crash occurs when this happens. Too often, these unfortunate drivers passed on quickly to the other world.

Today, you will find three-lane highways on hills so that climbing motorists can pass slower vehicles. These climbing lanes work well. Typically, the people in the descending lane have a solid line on their side and are prohibited from passing. Drivers in states that do allow downhill passing, like Colorado, are cautioned to watch for other drivers. Downhill passing can create a very dangerous situation for out-of-state drivers trying to pass in the uphill lane. They are not expecting a vehicle coming at them in their passing lane! In this sense, it becomes a dangerous three-lane highway.

Identify High-Accident Locations

And now for some ideas: Do you know that crash data is gathered, recorded, and charted by those who maintain our highways? What comes to mind is a map of city streets with pins marking accident locations. The data is used primarily for redesigning or otherwise improving the most dangerous locations in rural areas as well. In some places this information will be used to erect yellow advisory signs that carry messages such as "Dangerous Intersection Ahead" or "Sharp Curves." But so far, there are no signs delineating other high accident areas or the location of numerous highway deaths.

In recent years, we citizens have been allowed to mark these locations on our own. Our markers vary from a simple cross or a plastic wreath draped over a guardrail to elaborate shrines with photos and histories of the deceased. We, as taxpayers, have paid to have this data collected, analyzed, and stored at considerable expense. Why not make it more readily available to us? All that is needed is a simple small black square with a white number on it showing the deaths at that location. For example, it could be made available to travel advisory services such as AAA, Garmin, and MapQuest so they could alert drivers that are new to an area. Special signs might be posted at the worst locations.

It must be remembered that some of these locations out on the open highway cannot be corrected and, like the example given of the car sinking in a deep pond, are only dangerous when people exceed the speed limit. Other locations like the new roundabout in our city have something like 30 minor accidents over a 12-month period. Motorists new to the area should know this, and those who use it daily must constantly remind themselves to be careful.

Dangerous Times To Drive

If you can, plan your own trips to avoid the most dangerous times to drive.

SATURDAY
The most dangerous day of the week by far is Saturday. On that day, the chances of a crash are 55 percent higher! On Sunday and Friday, the chances are 12 percent higher.

MIDNIGHT TO 3 A.M.
The most crashes occur between midnight and 3 a.m., due often to drunk drivers as well as darkness. The second most dangerous time is between 9 p.m. and midnight when the body's metabolism wants to shut down in anticipation of sleep.

DECEMBER
During December, the chances of having a crash are 22 percent higher than the average. In October they are 17 percent higher and in August, 13 percent higher.

Planning to drive on a Saturday night late in December? Remember our Rules of Three and reconsider, especially if Christmas Eve falls on a Saturday. Santa and his reindeer took to the air many years ago in order to avoid this dangerous driving time.

Directions

Perhaps the most well known driving directions were given by former New York Yankee baseball catcher, Yogi Berra. His last instruction to visitors was, "When you come to the fork in the road, take it." It seems that, unlike most other homes, his sat in between two highways and could be reached by either route.

Today there are many new ways to obtain or give directions. These include internet services such as MapQuest and systems that come with vehicles that allow you to punch in your destination and receive step-by-step instructions to reach it. One of the best is by Garmin. It gives you vocal instructions as you approach critical intersections. This is far less distracting than glancing down at a map display on your dashboard to pinpoint where to turn. If you don't have these available, here are some old-fashioned techniques:

Start Your Directions from a Well-Known Point
If, for example, you are giving directions to your home, start from a well-known or easily

reached point, such as a particular exit on a freeway. Identify it by exit number and tell in which direction you turn as you exit. You can save yourself a great deal of time if you prepare written instructions for reaching your home from the three or four most common directions that visitors will take. These can be posted next to the phone for transmitting verbally to delivery people, sent out by email, or photocopied for mailing to visitors beforehand.

Give Distance, Direction, and a Landmark for Each Turn

From your well-known point, identify the name or number of the highway that travelers should take and the direction that they should go. Provide them with the mileage to the next turn and each turn thereafter. Finally, provide them with an easily recognized landmark at each turn, the direction that they turn, and the new route name or number.

It may seem redundant to give both landmarks and distances. It turns out that some people prefer to locate turns using landmarks while others find distances more helpful. That is why it is best to give all possible information. Finally, clearly identify the destination point. If their trip will end at your house, for example, you might note its color, architectural style, the house number, and the side of the street that it is on. If you give directions verbally, have the person receiving them write them down and read them back to you.

As mentioned, cars are often equipped with compasses and global positioning systems these days so that you can simply give them the map coordinates of your house and let their computer provide directions! There are, however, some important tips if you don't have global positioning. First, check any mileages that you give. If you say "about X" miles, it creates a great deal of anxiety. Measure it and give the exact distance in tenths if you can. Check your landmarks from time to time. Subsequent coats of paint on houses and changes in the ownership of roadside businesses can result in stale directions that confuse visitors.

Instructions such as "turn left where the White Castle used to be" or "turn right two miles before the Exxon Station" are not helpful!

If Receiving Directions, Write Them Down!

Keep a pencil and paper in your glove compartment and write down instructions. Once written, read them back to the sender for verification. If route numbers, mileages, or the direction that you take at a particular turn are missing, ask for them.

The New Wave of Travel Information

Cell phone downloads are coming of age as a source of travel assistance. Google Maps is one of several popular tools for obtaining routes and travel times. Traffic.com is free and provides detailed traffic information. You also can use this service via email on your

PC. While it will get you around most of North America, the traffic updates currently are available for only fifty major cities. For overseas driving directions, AT&T, Inc. offers global coverage, GPS driving directions, real-time traffic alerts, and more. It is available to AT&T subscribers for a monthly charge.[6]

One new service ties together traffic, weather, and routing information with appointments listed in your phone calendar. Other emerging services even provide real-time videos of major intersections and local streets.[7] These should be looked at before you begin your trip, not while you're driving!

A smartphone's large screen, decent speaker, and variety of mounting kits make it a tempting navigation device. At the present time, numerous apps are available for smartphones. These are quickly becoming more appealing as they offer additional information and require less battery power.[8]

Pitfalls

Those who rely solely on MapQuest will be completely lost when they miss a turn. For this reason, you should always have a roadmap for each of the states that you will be in. Those of you who have navigation systems should be sure to clean out the data in them before you sell your car. A recent "Dear Abby" letter told of a person buying a used car with a navigation system. When they turned it on, the system gave them the previous owner's address and the addresses of his friends, his bank, his workplace, and every other place that he had ever gone![9]

Emergency Contacts

Whenever you go on a trip, designate someone as an emergency contact. Tell that person where you are going and as many details as possible. These include the time you are leaving and arriving and the route or mode of transportation that you are taking. If you are flying or going on a long vacation, you may consider providing your contact with your itinerary.

Third Party

When you are meeting someone, have a third party available that both of you can contact. If you both have cell phones, have each other's number. If one of you doesn't have a cell phone, or if there is no cell phone service where you are going, use the third party as your contact.

Backup Plan

You also may wish to formulate a backup plan. For example, let's say someone is driving to the airport to meet you, but you miss your flight. Now, what is your backup plan for being picked up at the airport? You may agree beforehand that your driver will wait for the next flight. Backup plans can eliminate panic attacks such as when I waited four hours at a city bus terminal for my fiancée while she waited for me at another bus terminal in the same city.

Being Polite
Call your hosts early if plans change. And always call them at least 15 minutes before you arrive.

HOV Lanes

The term "HOV" stands for High Occupancy Vehicles. HOV lanes can be found on newer freeways as they approach downtown areas. The lanes are designed to promote carpooling and bus riding, thereby reducing peak hour traffic congestion. We are not talking clown cars here. Cars typically need as few as two occupants to be classified as an HOV. Often, the freeway will have a single HOV lane that is reversible, operating into the city in the morning rush hour and outbound during the evening. HOV lanes are most effective when combined with park-ride lots near suburban interchanges of the freeway. In some locations, drivers can pick up passengers without prearrangements. Drivers also have resorted to the use of dummies to qualify for entry into the lane. It is a source of glee for the officers who periodically station themselves at the HOV exit. There is a rumor that one officer even gives out two tickets, one to the driver and a second to the dummy.

Long Trips

If you are going on a long trip, it is helpful if you can have at least one other licensed driver accompany you. Then, you can take turns driving. Every two hours is a good time to stop and switch drivers. When you stop, take a short walk. It will refresh you.

Maintenance and Repairs
You will want to know that your car is in good condition before you begin a trip. But fewer and fewer drivers know about the internal workings of their cars. Nor are we aware of the many advances in the automobile industry. For example, batteries now can last the life of the car and tires will last fifty thousand miles instead of five thousand. The best plan for keeping your car in running shape is to perform all the routine maintenance recommended for your car in its owner's manual.

However, you might consider overriding the service department if their advice is to change your oil every five thousand miles. Changing your engine oil every three thousand miles is often recommended if you wish to own your car for a long period of time. Changing your oil every three thousand miles can be a matter of convenience as well. Manufacturers recommend that you rotate your tires every six thousand miles. If you take your car in for a three-thousand-mile oil change you can have them rotate the tires as well every second visit.

Of course if you plan to keep your car for only two hundred thousand miles, then, by all means change your oil every five thousand miles. That's what those fascinating fellows on the National Public Radio show, "Car Talk," recommend. If you use a good synthetic oil, you can even go 10,000 miles between oil changes. If you have a hybrid, check your manual for the recommended mileage between oil changes.

Mirrors

Ray Harroun, a race-car driver, invented the rearview mirror in 1911. He did it so that he could compete in the Indianapolis Speedway race without a riding mechanic.[10] Before then, all auto racers needed a riding mechanic to maintain engine oil levels and keep a lookout for overtaking competitors.

Mirrors have assisted all kinds of vehicle operators to get a better view without unnecessary discomfort or strain. Another person from that bygone era before the rearview mirror was Eddie Rickenbacker, America's most successful World War I flying ace. He downed 26 enemy planes. Rickenbacker credited his success with being able to see behind him as well as ahead. To do this, he constantly twisted his neck from side to side. During his first days on patrol, Rickenbacker continuously turned his head during the most difficult dives, spins, and corkscrew turns. He recounted in later life that it was this training that saved his life time and time again. It often enabled him to detect enemy planes before they could attack. But he kept throwing up as he did this. At first the ground crews dreaded his return to the ground because of all the barf in his fighter's cockpit. However, his nausea eventually disappeared.[11]

When to Use Mirrors
Fortunately for us, cars have three rearview mirrors. Two of these are referred to as side-view mirrors and are designed to show us what is behind our car on either side. We should position them correctly before we begin driving. And, we should glance at them periodically to see what is coming up behind us, especially when we halt at a light or stop sign. These are the occasions when we are most likely to be rear-ended. However, it's a good idea to check continuously. Also, we need to practice looking to the side. See the section in Chapter 6 entitled "Looking out for Other Cars." For a good view even with a stiff neck, we can initiate the turn with the torso, then turn the neck.

How to Adjust Mirrors
Drivers typically adjust their side-view mirrors so that they can just see the sides of their car when they are sitting in the normal driving position. Interestingly, the right side-view mirror on North American cars is curved, as are mirrors on European cars. Objects in the

curved mirror are closer than they appear. The curved mirror requires little or no adjustment for different drivers.

There is a way to set your driver-side mirror so that you can cut down on the blind spot on that side. Sitting in the driver's seat, put the side of your head against the left side window, then adjust the mirror so that you can just see the side of the car. To check the setting, watch a vehicle passing in the left lane while you are seated in the normal driving position. It should appear in the outside mirror before its image leaves the rearview mirror and, it should appear in your peripheral vision before its image leaves the outside mirror.

For the right outside mirror, sit in the driver's seat and lean to the right to position your head at the car's centerline. Then, adjust the mirror so that you can just see the car's side. These adjustments, if done correctly, can make it unnecessary to take your vision off the road in front of you when you turn to look to the side. But do check to the side until you are assured that these settings work for you.[12]

Mirror sizes vary widely. The area of the side-view mirror on my minivan is 45 square inches while the area of the side-view mirror on my friend's 1999 BMW M3 Roadster is only 21 square inches. Police officers and professional race drivers use a rearview mirror with a 180-degree field of vision rather than the 52 degrees available with a "standard" mirror. These wider mirrors clip over your existing mirror and are available in specialty catalogs.[13] You also can buy small, round, convex mirrors and attach them to your side-view mirror.

If you are driving in Europe, be aware that both side mirrors are convex. In the United States only the passenger's side-view mirror is convex.[14]

Adjust Your Headrest

Other things to do to reduce the danger from rear-end collisions include making sure that your seat headrest is high enough to catch the back of your head.

Keep Your Wheels Straight

Also, if stopped while waiting to make a left turn, do not turn your wheels until you actually start the turn. If your car has a manual transmission, consider taking the car out of gear. Otherwise, a rear-end collision could propel your car into the oncoming lane of traffic.

Blind Spot Warning Systems

Some new cars offer blind spot warning systems. One example activates a light in the upper left corner of your left side mirror when a vehicle is lurking in your blind spot. Systems also can sound an alert if you switch on the turn signal when there's an adjacent vehicle. These usually work well and provide a valuable assist when you are moving over to the lane to your left.[15]

Numbering Highways

Numbered highways orient us to our location. Numbers are used on the Interstate System, on other federal highways, and on state and county roads. Cities and towns use numbers as well as names for streets and avenues. It is useful to know the systems behind these numbers even if you resort to Garmin or MapQuest to plan your trips.

Because of their cross-country nature, the Interstate System of Defense Highways is perhaps the most familiar to most people. The odd-numbered interstates run north and south. They start with I-5 on the west coast and end with I-95 on the East Coast. The even-numbered interstates run east and west and go from I-4 in Florida to I-94 in the north.

A strange anomaly is the island of Oahu in the state of Hawaii. It has three interstates, H-1, H-2, and H-3. None of them connect to another state, but they still can be designated interstates because they serve purposes of national defense.

Supplemental interstates have three digits. The first digit identifies the type of route and the last two identify the primary interstate that that route serves. For example, I-270 serves as a feeder between Washington, D.C., and I-70 northwest of that city. The 400s are generally reserved for circular bypasses of cities. Thus, I-465 is a circular bypass route around Indianapolis that connects to I-65 on both the north and south sides of that city. You will find identically numbered three-digit interstates in more than one city. For example there is an I-495 around both Boston and Washington, D.C. If you go to the San Francisco Bay area you will find I-280, 380, 580, 680, 780, 880, and 980, all with connections to I-80. But there is no loop highway there, so there is no I-480. No wonder we use GPS systems today.

The other major highways in this country are part of the previous federal highway system. As such they also have odd numbers for north-south routes and even numbers for east-west. For example, US Route 1 runs down the East Coast and US Route 2 goes near the northern border of our country. States and counties have numbered routes as well, and most cities have numbered streets. Perhaps one of the most understandable and easily navigable cities is Manhattan. Here the streets and avenues are arranged in a grid pattern and both are numbered. Of course, even here there are exceptions. While everyone knows that Avenue of the Americas is really Sixth Avenue, they can get confused because York, Lexington, and Park Avenue are not numbered. That's when MapQuest and global positioning systems can come in handy.

Progressive Timing of Traffic Lights

Progressive timing is a strategy for moving traffic more efficiently. In progressive timing, traffic lights are set to turn green ahead of you as you move along the street at a constant speed. Progressive timing is frequently used on one-way streets.

A well-known example of progressive timing on one-way streets is the north-south avenues in New York City. Unfortunately, in New York City, queues from cross streets often back up onto these avenues. And, the avenues themselves can be filled with vehicles that are double and triple parked. Such impediments often hinder the functioning of Manhattan's one-way avenues.

In some regions, progressive timing also is used on two-way highways that connect the suburbs to downtown areas. The timing is set to favor the heavier direction of flow, inbound traffic in the morning and outbound flows during the afternoon. In these situations, the reverse flows will be delayed.

Ramp Metering

Ramp metering is a strategy for reducing peak hour bottlenecks on freeways. Very simply, there is a traffic signal on each entrance ramp. It turns to green when space on the freeway becomes available. There also may be an automatic gate opposite the light. Persons first encountering these lights and gates will see gaps on the freeway and wonder why the light is red and the gate is closed. It is because a certain number of gaps are required to keep the traffic flowing.

Regional Differences

I can vividly remember the first time that I drove in downtown Boston. It seemed that from every driveway and side street zoomed a driver intent on cutting me off. Years later I moved from the rural Midwest to New England. It was then that I realized that I was used to traveling at much greater speeds than native New Englanders. The Bostonians were "zooming" out of side streets because they were used to people on the through street driving more slowly.

The populous states in New England have more small towns with low speed limits than the Midwest. At the speeds I was used to, such invasion of the roadway ahead of me called for slamming on my brakes. At these lower speeds, a Bostonian can safely maneuver their car into a gap in the traffic that is so short that it horrified me. That is a regional difference that takes some getting used to, especially with the New Englander's penchant for avoiding the use of turn signals. Beware; a few of these Bostonians may try to avail themselves of these short gaps on express highways like the Massachusetts Turnpike.

On a more positive note, drivers in Pittsburgh have adopted a very courteous practice described as a "Pittsburgh Left." Streets in older residential areas are too narrow for left turn lanes. At these intersections, drivers wishing to turn left must wait a considerable time while the straight through traffic clears the intersection. When the light changes, Pittsburgh motorists often allow the first car or two facing them to turn left in front of them before they cross the intersection.

Somewhat more notorious is the "Pittsburgh Chair." With parking limited in these residential areas, homeowners often leave a chair in the parking space in front of their home until they return. Vacant baby carriages and potted plants also have been spotted reserving these preferred parking spots.

A recent news item states that New York City has supplanted Miami as the U.S. city with the angriest and most aggressive drivers. Dallas/Fort Worth came in second, followed by Detroit, Atlanta, and Minneapolis/St. Paul. Miami ranked a distant seventh. The survey noted that Cleveland and Portland (Oregon) were voted to have the most courteous, considerate drivers. And Baltimore, Sacramento, and Pittsburgh rounded out the top five cities for the most pleasant drivers.[16]

Are there other regional differences? For example, you might hesitate a little longer at traffic lights in Florida or Arizona. In the past, these states were sometimes noted for motorists who run red lights. Or, maybe you take secondary roads to avoid those one-second gaps between vehicles on Los Angeles freeways. And, when you go to Arizona, Montana, Texas, or Wyoming you may feel uncomfortable with our advice to move at the same speed as the surrounding traffic—it is fast!

And, you *should* know how things go down in Washington, D.C. This is the deal: Every day of every week a different conference is scheduled, a different organization is calling in regional personnel, and a different group of foreign dignitaries is arriving. All but the most prominent of these temporary guests have rented a car at one of the three airports nearby. And each is learning how to drive on Washington's streets. Those who are there for a week or so will tell you that the location of rush hour traffic jams changes each day as the newest arrivals zero in on a new and different destination. As these folks drive, they are trying to find the shift lever, headlight switch, mirror controls, and windshield wiper switch on their rental car. Chaos and inattentiveness are the norm. Much additional chaos occurs at night or in rain or snow, particularly if it is a group from a place such as the Philippines who have never seen snow or a lobbyist from Hong Kong who is used to driving on the opposite side of the road.

Perhaps the most dangerous situation is when a driver from one section of our country is tooling down the highway in another state. Such would be a Los Angeles freeway driver on a winding New England country road. I will leave the rest to your imagination.

Rental Cars

Are you going on a trip? Recently I exited an Amtrak train at the West Glacier stop in Glacier Park, Montana. About the only thing there besides a small station was my rental car. And, it had a cracked windshield! So it's important to do a walk-around before getting in your rental. It had been driven to the station from a nearby agency. I called the rental company and had them note the problem before I started to drive. You should request another car if your inspection reveals any of the following:[17]

- Badly worn tires.
- Malfunctioning windshield wipers, lights, and heater or a/c depending on the season.
- Soft brakes. Hit them hard before you exit the lot.
- A dirty interior. This includes bad smells.
- A weak battery. Pop the hood and look for green corrosion on the battery terminals.
- High mileage. Rental agencies sold their cars at 38,700 miles in 2011 as compared to 26,100 miles in 2007. (One customer asks for a replacement car if he is offered one with over thirty thousand miles. While not a lot of miles, having had at least 30 or 40 different drivers takes its toll on the vehicle.)

If the rental agency claims there are no other cars in your category, ask for a free upgrade. If this doesn't work, advise the agency that you will wait until a better car is turned in.[18] Some experienced travelers always order a mini-subcompact. More often than not, the rental agency is out of them when they arrive so they get a free upgrade.

When you walk around the car, make sure that any dents are noted on your rental agreement. Once inside the car, take a few moments to get familiar with the controls. They may be in different locations or they may work differently than those on your car. It is important to know before you encounter an emergency. If you can, rent the same model car as the one that you own to eliminate this problem.

Right-Of-Way

At a four-way intersection with a stop sign at all four approaches, the car that arrives at the intersection first has the right-of-way. The question arises amongst lawyers and others as to who has the right-of-way when two cars arrive simultaneously. Driver manuals will say that the person on the right has the right-of-way and may proceed first.

Things get a little more confusing when two cars arrive simultaneously and are stopped across from each other. In this instance, courtesy is required on the part of one of the drivers. That is why you may see that driver blinking his lights or waving at you to go ahead. It's the proactive driver who is waving and the defensive driver who goes first. That is an interesting turn of events, eh?

A more clear-cut rule is that a left-turning vehicle must yield to oncoming traffic. And if the street that you are on is the only one with a stop sign you must yield to through traffic approaching the intersection.

There are many other instances where there may be a question as to who has the right-of-way. One example is a two-lane highway. As you are driving along, you come upon a fuel delivery truck that is stopped and is partially blocking your lane. To get around the truck, you must use the oncoming lane. Contrary to the opinion of some, you *do not* have the right to occupy that lane unless it is free. In other words, if a car is approaching from the other direction, it has the right to the clear lane. Hey, it's her lane!

Seat Belts and Flying Objects

As of this writing, New Hampshire is still the only state in the country in which it is legal for adult drivers to not wear seat belts. I happened to hear a legislator from that state speaking on Public Radio with pride about how if they had voted in an adult seat belt law it would have saved *only* five lives the previous year.

I am not sure where he came upon that statistic. The official New Hampshire Driver's Manual states that 108 persons who were not wearing seat belts (safety restraints) died in accidents inside vehicles in a recent year. It goes on to say that 55 of those victims would have been alive today if they had been belted up. I know that if I were a New Hampshire legislator, I couldn't sleep at night with the weight of "just five" deaths on my conscience. But then again, the state's motto is "Live Free or Die."

Always Wear Your Seat Belt
Seat belts usage is now at 83 percent nationwide. In 14 states and the nation's capital, usage is over 90 percent. The highest usage is found in Michigan and Hawaii (97 percent), while the lowest is in Massachusetts where fewer than 67 percent buckle up.[19] Wearing seat belts has saved hundreds of thousands of lives and helped to reduce the country's highway fatality rate. Since most accidents happen close to home, seat belts should always be worn, even during short trips. Some believe that they are not needed with air bags. That is not true. Air bags can cause lethal injuries if seat belts are not fastened.

How to Buckle Seat Belts
When buckling up, be sure that the straps are flat and firmly in contact with your body. The lower strap should be around your abdomen and the upper strap around your chest. Also keep your seat back in an upright position and make sure that there is at least a 10-inch clearance between your chest and the steering wheel.[20] Other positions or loose belts can cause serious injury if you are in a crash. If you are an unusually large or small person, special adjustments may be needed. Find out what these are.

Always Strap Infants in Approved Seats
Some brands of infant seats can be difficult to attach. Don't purchase yours unless you are first shown how to install it properly. Currently, it is recommended that they be placed in rear seats. See the section of Chapter 6 entitled "Children and Car Seats."

Damaged Seatbelts

Replace frayed or damaged seatbelts, or a nonfunctioning buckle or take-up mechanism immediately. These should be replaced by your dealer at no cost while the vehicle is under warranty.

Insist That All of Your Passengers Wear Seat Belts

Most passengers understand the need to wear a seat belt if they are sitting in front. However, it is a common misconception that people in the rear seats do not need to wear seat belts. Statistics indicate that seat belt compliance is indeed significantly lower for rear-seat passengers. It is a bad decision on their part because occupants who don't wear seat belts are often flung from the car in an accident, whether sitting in the front or back. This type of injury is often fatal. And, if rear-seat occupants are not hurled from the car, they often crash into the driver and passengers, causing extensive injuries to both. A video demonstrating this can be found online at YouTube by entering "Rear Passenger Seatbelt" in the search window. It's a graphic short film that shows an unbuckled rear-seat passenger killing all three of the other occupants of the car during a collision.

Flying Objects

What if you haven't secured the loose objects in your car? If you are in a crash, they will keep flying at your initial speed until they hit something. A tissue box weighing half a pound would feel like a 30-pound object if it hits you during a rapid deceleration from 60 miles per hour.[21]

But that may be the least of your worries. Check also for loose wrenches, skis, tire jacks, and bottles. They are just a few of the heavier items that can cause severe head injuries and puncture wounds if left loose in a car. Particularly dangerous are heavy or sharp objects on the dashboard or rear window shelf. Only recently have some auto manufacturers been offering tie down facilities for larger cargo. When possible, use your trunk, roof rack, or rooftop carrier for such items (Note that putting items on the roof will reduce your gas mileage).

Signs and Pavement Markings

Most of you will recall from your driving test that there are three types of signs, Regulatory, Warning, and Guide. Signs are an extremely important help to us in the first of the three steps in proactive driving, scouting the road ahead. Often, with merely a glance, we can update ourselves on the current speed limit, prepare for a curve in the road ahead, or undertake many other driver actions. Here is a quick review of a few of these signs to refresh your memory for when you next take a drive.

Regulatory Signs

Regulatory signs tell drivers what they can or cannot do. These signs are red, black on white or white on black. Red is used for eight-sided "stop" signs, triangular "yield" signs and square "do not enter" signs.

Other regulatory signs are vertical rectangles—taller than they are wide. These signs show turning restrictions, lane use, speed limits, or pedestrian and parking control. A red circle with a red slash on any of these signs means "No." Other examples include no parking at bus stops, the weight limit of a bridge, or the location of a railroad crossing.

International road signs are sometimes different. One helpful example is the stop signs in Canada. They include a generalized diagram of the intersection and an indication of which other approaches also have stop signs.

Warning Signs

Warning signs are yellow and tell you what to expect a short distance ahead. They are diamond-shaped. Examples include:

Merge	Two-way traffic	Dip in road
Intersection	Pedestrian crossing	Slippery pavement
Changes in lane width	Deer crossing	Curves

Other shapes are used for railroad crossings (round), school zones (five-sided in the shape of a house), and pennant-shaped for no-passing zones.

Guide Signs

Guide signs include green signs for destinations and mileage, blue signs for roadside service, and brown signs for recreational areas.
Mile Markers

Mile markers (green signs with white letters) can be helpful, especially if you want to report the site of a crash. In Vermont for example, the top line denotes the route number. The middle line identifies the town and county number and the bottom line indicates the mileage from the town line in a south to north or west to east direction.[22] Find out how to read these in your state.

Signs and Signing Practices Vary from State to State

One example that comes to mind is the treatment of "no passing" zones. The first of three adjoining New England states relies solely on the two yellow centerlines to guide motorists. Passing is permitted only if the centerline on your side is dashed, and is prohibited when the line on your side is continuous again.

The second state adds a yellow pennant-shaped sign on the left side of the road where the dashed line ends. The sign reads "No Passing Zone." I've always wondered if out-of-state motorists understand that they are supposed to read and obey signs that are on the other side of the road.

The third state uses the pennant-shaped sign's same message, "No Passing Zone," and puts a rectangular sign across from it on the right side of the road. That sign is white and reads "Do Not Pass."

In a fourth state, Georgia, that same sign on the right side of the road reads "No Passing When Solid Line Is Right of Centerline." Fortunately, most drivers understand these message variations.

Signs and Older Drivers

The size of lettering on signs is large enough to give a person with good eyesight enough time to act. However, as we grow older, we may lose some of our visual acuity and may not be able to read signs as quickly. It is particularly true at night. This may cause us to drive past our exit on a freeway. It is why older drivers should ask their passenger to help read the signs. If you do miss an exit, continue on to the next. It is extremely dangerous to back up on a freeway.

Poor eyesight can be dangerous in many other situations as well. For example, you may be planning a left turn but must hit the brakes to do so because you couldn't read the street sign in time. In this situation, continue straight ahead, turn off at the next intersection and backtrack.

Larger signs are appearing. For instance, the 55 miles per hour speed limit signs on US 101 in Oregon are four feet high with 20-inch high numerals. The more common height for this sign is 30 inches with 10-inch high numerals. Another example is on US 2 approaching Boston. On this highway, the speed limit, route numbers, and exit sign lettering all are large and easily visible.

Pavement Markings

Lines, lettering, and symbols on the pavement are used along with highway signs and signals. These markings most often are yellow or white. Sometimes they are reflective. Examples include traffic lane markings, pedestrian crosswalks, vehicle stop lines, no passing zones, and directional arrows.

The most important pavement markings are the yellow centerlines described in a previous paragraph. Either single or double lines are used to separate traffic traveling in opposite directions. Broken yellow centerlines mean you may pass when safe. As previously stated, you may not pass when a solid line is on your side of the center of the road. You may pass if there is a broken line on your side of the center of the road and there are no oncoming cars.

White lines separate traffic lanes traveling in the same direction. You are not supposed to change lanes if the lines are solid. White lines also mark pedestrian crosswalks and stop lines and identify the right edge of the road.

In New England, you may be driving along a main road that comes to a confusing intersection with four or even five exiting streets. To find which is the main road, look for the one with the double yellow centerline.

In Europe, you may find white centerlines and there may be no lines marking the right side of the travelway.

Additional Information

Pamphlets describing road signs, signals, and markings can be obtained from the American Automobile Association or your state motor vehicle bureau.[23] It is highly recommended that you review one of these pamphlets periodically to refresh your memory as to the exact meaning of these items. Also see the sections in Chapter 6 entitled "Stop Signs" and "Traffic Lights."

Tires

Tires have been dramatically improved in recent years, thanks, in part, to improvements to NASCAR tires. Today's tires offer increased safety and endurance. Some will even maintain inflation when punctured. Usually a tire that lasts twice as long does not cost twice as much, suggesting that those who can afford it should purchase good tires.

Use Good Quality Steel-Belted Radials

The design of combination mud and snow tires has improved to the point that they work well year-round in most northern climates, eliminating the hassle of keeping a separate set of snow tires for winter. If you are unsure of what tires to buy, there are plenty of sources for good advice. A most interesting one is rural letter carriers. If yours is friendly, you might ask her opinion. The right side tires on their cars suffer el primo abuse. No wonder warranty people at tire dealers run out the back door when a rural carrier walks in the front.

Maintain Proper Tire Pressure

Tires can lose 1 psi (pound per square inch) of pressure per month under normal conditions. They also can lose 1 psi for every 10 degrees Fahrenheit of temperature drop.[24]

Using Run-Flat and "Doughnut" Tires

A relatively recent development in tire safety is "run-flat" tires. These eliminate the need to change a tire in the middle of the night, in bad weather, or on the shoulder of a busy highway. You can drive 50 or more miles on them, thus allowing you to reach a garage.[25] Run-flat tires should not be confused with the "doughnut" or undersized spare tires with which manufacturers sometimes equip cars. These also are good for a short distance. But you have to put them on first.

In both cases, you should consider purchasing a full-sized spare tire. The smaller tires are a convenience to a manufacturer but an inconvenience to you and, possibly, a safety hazard depending upon how far or fast you have to drive after you change to the spare. Most manufacturers do offer a mounting kit if you decide to add a spare to your car or change the one you have to a full-sized tire.

Visually Check Inflation Before Driving
Always visually check tire inflation before driving as part of your vehicle walk-around.

Measure and Adjust Pressure in All Tires in Spring and Fall
The most important times to check tire pressure are in the spring and fall. If you put in enough air to reach 30 pounds of pressure in July, you will find that the tire pressure will be less in January even if the tire doesn't leak. For this reason, you should check and adjust your tire pressures at least twice a year, on the first really hot day in the spring and on the first really cold day in the fall. Because of the previously mentioned slow loss of pressure, it is even better if drivers check their tire pressure with a gauge once a month or each time that the car is serviced. While newer cars may have pressure sensors installed that will signal even an annoyingly small discrepancy in tire pressure, it is still important as a proactive driver to know the recommended psi. Don't forget to check the spare as well!

Maintain a Safe Tread Depth
"Bald tires are unsafe." Most people have heard this but some may not understand why. The smooth surface on these tires provides nowhere for water or snow to go, so the tire hydroplanes very easily. Obviously, applying brakes to a hydroplaning car is like shouting "Stop!" at an avalanche.

Thus, a badly worn tread reduces your ability to stop your car quickly. In recognition of this, most state laws specify a minimum safe tread depth, typically 1/16 of an inch. This is the tread thickness if you can put a penny in the tread and see the top of Lincoln's head.[26] However, tests by *Consumer Reports* indicate an 8 percent drop in hydroplaning resistance and 15 percent less overall snow traction when tire treads are worn to 5/32 of an inch. Their recommendation is to start looking for tires when the tread is down to 1/8 of an inch. The test for that depth is George Washington's hairline on a quarter.

Rotate Your Tires
Rotating your tires can extend their life. Do so in accordance with the manufacturer's recommendations. Typically this is every five thousand to six thousand miles.

Observe and Correct Unusual Tire Wear

State laws require that tires be free of cuts, tears, and any other dangerous conditions. But uneven tread wear can be just as dangerous as bald tires. Uneven wear needs to be corrected by a tire specialist. It is, for example, an indication that the entire vehicle may be out of alignment. You can spot misalignment by going some distance behind your car and looking under it at the tires. If the rear tires are to one side of the front tires, you have a problem. Such a car may spin to the right in an emergency braking situation if the front tires line up to the left of the rear tires. In a used car such misalignment may indicate that the car has been involved in a major crash.

Have Your Tires Balanced

Out-of-balance tires develop flat spots or cups. This shortens their life and renders them less safe.

Tire Repairs

See the section of this chapter entitled "Before You Drive."

Travelway

Before you drive, you should know about that white line that separates the highway from the shoulder. It is the right-hand boundary of the "travelway." Even knowledgeable drivers may not know that it is illegal to drive to the right of that line. Often drivers will find a vehicle ahead of them that is stopped in their lane while waiting to make a left turn. As the following driver, they are sorely tempted to go to the right (onto the shoulder) to get past the waiting car. This can be a problem if an oncoming car also is waiting for a left turn. That driver may not be able to see you and you may not be able to see them. The reason? The car in front of you is blocking both his view and your view. Now, let's say that he makes his left turn at the same time that you pass the car in front of you on that car's right. There is really little time for either of you to react once you see each other.

The car in front of you also may be blocking your view of a pedestrian. And in some areas, there may be bike traffic to the right of that line. So *be very careful* if you think that you must leave the travelway. It is illegal and you will be at fault if there is an accident.

Uninsured Motorists

Insurance is not a driving skill. However, knowledge of how liability insurance works is important in today's world. There currently are about a half-dozen states that do not require motorists to carry bodily injury liability insurance. This insurance covers damages paid to another person for physical injuries to his or her person that are caused by a negligent driver. Even when this insurance is carried, it is easy to imagine that an injured person's bodily injuries will exceed the wrongdoer's policy limit.

No-fault insurance is used in some states, but the legally required coverage of this alternative also is often too low to pay for all the costs of any personal injuries that you may sustain in a serious accident caused by someone else. That is why it is extremely important that motorists carry uninsured motorist coverage. With this coverage the injured person's own policy will make up the difference between his or her damages and the wrongdoer's bodily injury policy limit. This coverage is inexpensive and is doubly important now as more drivers are dropping their bodily injury coverage and, in some instances, all their auto insurance.[27]

CHAPTER 6 – WHEN YOU ARE DRIVING

PAST SCHOOLHOUSES
TAKE IT SLOW
WE NEED TO LET
THE LITTLE SHAVERS GROW

Burma-Shave

All-Wheel Drive

There are three ways to move a vehicle forward, 1) front-wheel drive; 2) rear-wheel drive; and 3) all-wheel drive. Of these, all-wheel (four-wheel) drive provides the best road gripping abilities in most situations. Because it gives less gas mileage, it is sometimes offered "on-demand." In these cars, all-wheel drive is automatically engaged when needed. A few all-wheel drive vehicles have a control on the dashboard or floor so the driver can manually engage all wheels.

Animals in the Car

Animals are not people. But it's hard to tell that when Bowser is sitting alertly in the passenger seat of a pickup thoroughly enjoying the passing scenery. This particular Fido is well trained. He is holding still and looking ahead. Not all pets are as perfect. Part of proactive driving is preparing for a safe trip before you leave the house. This emphatically includes making sure that any animal in your car is under control.

When Driving, Have Pets Under Control

I have seen huge dogs roving from side to side in the front seat of a car, alternately sticking their head out of one window or the other. In the process they are leaping across the driver's lap and blocking his view. In other cases, I have seen tiny pooches sitting in the driver's lap. One arm of the driver is actually petting the dog as she is driving. In the movie, "Marley and Me," Marley, the mischievous Labrador retriever, leans so far out the window that, well, you have to see the movie. The distractions that an uncontrolled animal create can result in driver inattention and lead to a crash.

Cats are another matter. Many are extremely susceptible to motion sickness. One of their favorite spots to hide is at the driver's feet. Attempting to step on the brake and stepping on the cat instead will make your life both interesting and dangerous. Another favorite tactic of cats is to suddenly cling to your thighs or shoulders with claws extended. While the cat may be the boss in the house, you must let that feline know that the car is your domain.

The best way to control a dog or cat is to keep them in a cage (or carrier) in the car. This may save the animal if you are involved in a crash. You also can train a dog to sit quietly, particularly if you keep your windows rolled up. Recently some folks in New York State wanted to require dogs riding in the back of pickup trucks to be on a short leash. That is probably a good idea with or without a law.

Leaving Animals in Your Vehicle (Illegal in Some States)
When left alone in the car, Marley chewed the upholstery to smithereens. However, most dogs will just sit in the driver's seat and wait. That is where the scent of their owner is strongest. In any event, have water available for them to drink, leave a window cracked for air, and never leave them in a vehicle in hot weather.

Approaching a Car with a Dog Inside
When alone in a vehicle, most dogs imagine themselves in a cave. If approached by a stranger, they will feel challenged and become aggressive. That is why it is not a good idea to reach your hand through the window of a stranger's car to pet the cute doggie.

Animals on the Road

Every year there are over five hundred thousand car/animal collisions in the United States.[1] Decisions when encountering an animal on the road are not clear-cut and vehicle damage is quite likely if a medium to large animal is hit.

Hitting a Small Animal
Even the safest of drivers is likely to run into a dog, cat, squirrel, or chipmunk over a lifetime behind the wheel. The reason is that some of these animals have no road sense and will dash in front of us without thinking. It is sad and the pet owners will grieve their loss. So please stop and tell them what has happened if you hit a dog or cat. If the owners are not available, report the incident to the local police within 24 hours. This is a law (for dogs) in some states and is a good idea for any animal that you hit.

The Turkey Factor
Turkeys tend to cross the road at any time of day. Of course, it could be a pheasant, a child, or any number of other things. But I like turkeys. They are not required by the FAA to file flight plans, so they take off whenever they feel like it. In fact, their first reaction upon seeing you is flight. However, they always seem to be pointed across the road, so that is where

their flight will take them. During takeoff and the initial 30 feet of flight, they are struggling for altitude and have all the maneuverability of a bowling bowl with hummingbird wings. Their bulky nature dictates a low angle of initial flight, one that when starting from the left side of the road will bring them to the height of your windshield as they cross in front of you. It's good news if they don't come through the windshield and "merely" obliterate your line of sight. Bad news is when they break the windshield and land in your face. In any event, you need to brake instantly when you see a turkey. You may have driven 40 years without a similar situation, but you still must be alert and ready. It is that distraction of a nanosecond that can be fatal (for you and the turkey).

Avoiding a Major Crash

It may sound cruel, but someday you may have to decide between staying in your lane and hitting an animal or swerving into the oncoming lane and inviting a head-on crash. If there is no traffic, and your speed is not too great, you can change lanes to miss the animal. Otherwise, your best solution is to stand on the brakes, providing there is not an 18-wheeler right behind you. Think about this type of situation beforehand and decide on your strategies so you'll be ready. Just remember, other drivers are not expecting you to enter their lane or go into an emergency braking situation.

The Infamous White-tailed Deer

This brings us to the subject of white-tailed deer, the auto's mortal enemy. As the proactive driver looking down the road, you may see a car ahead swerve to miss a deer. Hopefully, you can slow in time to avoid the bounding beast. These animals are not so big that a collision with one necessarily means a catastrophe. However, they can come through the windshield if hit head on. And, about 150 drivers did die last year from deer/auto crashes.[2] Therefore it may be better to brake hard even if the deer that you see passes safely in front of your car. The reason? There may be a second or third deer on the way!

My recent experience occurred at night on an interstate. I was traveling at 65 miles per hour when the 18-wheeler ahead of me hit a deer and pulled to the shoulder. Because it was dark, I didn't see what happened until the deer passed under the truck and revealed itself in front of my minivan. It seemed to me that a sudden swerve could flip my vehicle, so I elected to straddle the deer. My vehicle had enough clearance to do this but by driving over the deer the gas tank was damaged. Fortunately for the car, it was a very slow leak and there was no fire.

That deer are a major problem was demonstrated to me most recently while driving in New Brunswick, Canada, on TransCanada Route 2. High fences had been constructed along both sides of the highway. And, perhaps in an admission that some deer would even get by these, special deer "turnstiles" were provided at strategic intervals. These allowed deer to exit the highway but not enter.

There are devices on the market that attach to the front bumper of your car and produce a high-pitched sound that is supposed to alert deer to your approach. That may be worth a try if you live in deer country. As it stands, more deer are being killed by drivers than by hunters!

Moose and Other Very Large Animals

What we have in mind here are the ultimate road kill disasters: moose, mule deer, elk, bears, and cattle. A moose, for example, is so long-legged that when you knock its legs out from under it, the body will come through your windshield. It's best to slow down when you drive through the areas that these animals inhabit. They are most active around dawn and dusk and during the autumn mating season. Cars have been charged by moose, so avoid beeping. Pull off the road, stop, and extinguish your headlights. If the moose is standing in the middle of the highway, wait until it leaves.

ATVs and Snowmobiles

All terrain vehicles (ATVs) and snowmobiles are intended for off-road operation. Conflicts with cars occur when they cross a road or highway to get from one off-road location to another. One afternoon several years ago, my wife was driving through our subdivision at 20 miles per hour. Unknown to her, a teenage boy had just returned from high school and was determined to take his brand new ATV out onto the highway before his parents returned home from work. His driveway sat down from the road and a car parked along the side of the street shielded the drive from the view of passing motorists. He gunned the ATV to make it up the drive, zoomed onto the road without looking and impacted the right front fender of my wife's compact wagon. The collision knocked out one of her headlights and severely damaged the ATV. The kid was ejected from the ATV and flew head first over the car. She was still shaking when I got home two hours later. Miraculously the teen was not seriously injured.

These vehicles can cross the road in front of you at any time. And, the drivers may be inexperienced operators. Look for them in suburban and rural areas and be prepared. In winter, you can often a see a trail of snow on the pavement where the snowmobiles have crossed the road.

Last winter a teenage girl was driving a snowmobile for the first time. As she approached the highway outside of our town, she saw a car coming and attempted to slow down. Being unfamiliar with the vehicle, she accelerated instead and crashed into the car. The snowmobile was totaled and she was killed.

Sometimes ATVs and snowmobiles are operated on the highway even if it is illegal. If you come upon one traveling along the road, pass carefully as the driver, unaware of your presence, may dart onto a trail on the left side of the highway.

Backing Up

Vehicles are more difficult to back up out of driveways and parking spaces today because of styling changes. These changes have reduced the window glass in the rear of the car, and otherwise reduced driver visibility. For this reason, you should avoid backing up your car when there are obstacles behind you. This "rule" applies even if your car has a rear-mounted camera. If it is necessary, try to back up the shortest distance possible before moving forward again. Back out of a parking space slowly and in the same direction that you went in. As you do so, turn on your flashers. To read more, see the upcoming section entitled "Blind Spots."

Bicyclists

The number of bicycles on the streets and roads is growing daily. The same traffic rules and regulations apply to both cars and bicyclists. However, bicycles are less visible, especially at night. Be on the lookout for bikes as you scout ahead. Extra caution is needed as you approach bicyclists because their speed is so much different from yours. And, the slightest mistake on either of your parts can cause serious injury to the rider. Slow your car as you come up to a bicyclist and do not pass until it is safe. When you do pass, leave at least three feet of space between the right side of your car and the bicycle. Also learn to recognize and respect specially designated bike lanes.

Some of the common crashes with bicycles occur when motorists turn left without noticing an oncoming rider. Or, they turn right at an intersection without first checking for a bicyclist to their right who is continuing straight ahead. Another cause of car/bike crashes is the motorist who opens his car door as a rider approaches.[3]

Blind Pedestrians

It is not often that we motorists interact directly with the visually impaired. The most likely spot is at an intersection where a blind person is attempting to cross. We are alerted to the blind through the presence of a white cane with red bands around the bottom. The blind person may be accompanied by a guide dog. Some folks are visually impaired but can use their remaining vision to help them cross the street. The important thing for motorists is to come to a complete stop before the crosswalk. This is particularly critical if you are turning right on red. The blind pedestrian is counting on the sound of your vehicle stopping before he or she crosses the street. What is not helpful is honking or yelling at the visually impaired, or anyone else for that matter.[4]

Blind Spots

Blind spots are defined as areas that you can't see when you sit in the driver's seat of your car. To avoid accidents, be aware of these and know those spaces around your car that you can't see in your mirrors. Below are some of the most notorious.

Before Driving, Walk Around Your Car

If you sit in your car when it is in the driveway, you will notice that you can't see directly behind it, or along the passenger side. You can't even see directly in front of it. Do an experiment. Have a friend slowly walk around the car with a piece of chalk and outline the "footprint" inside of which his feet disappear from view in your windshield and mirrors. You will be surprised. It is a *very* large space. For this reason, it is good to walk around your car before starting (also mentioned in the section in Chapter 5 entitled "Before You Drive").

While Driving, Check the Areas to the Side Before Changing Lanes

As you are driving on a freeway, you may notice that you can't see a car in your mirror if the car is opposite you. Therefore, it is necessary to actually turn your head and look to your left and behind you before you change lanes. (See "Looking Out for Other Cars" in Chapter 6.) In this situation, you can often hear a vehicle even though you don't see it. Avoiding loud music or cell phone conversations gives you an important margin of safety for this blind spot.

And, as a driver of an overtaking car, watch the car you are passing. If it appears that its driver doesn't see you and is turning into your lane, slow down and beep your horn.

Check Carefully Before Turning

The left and right windshield pillars create blind spots. This is especially important to take into account when you are making a left turn.

Trucks and Other Large Vehicles Have Blind Spots

Trucks and other large vehicles have even bigger blind spots. As a matter of fact, the driver of a large truck cannot see you at all if you tailgate. Instead, stay far enough back so that you can see the driver's side-view mirror. Avoid passing a large truck on the right as they may not be looking for an overtaking car on that side of their rig.

Before Parking, Locate the Corners of Your Car

Parallel parking involves tight clearances. Typically, the law requires that you park your vehicle within one foot of the curb. To help you do this, have someone stand at each corner of your car before you drive it the first time so you can understand exactly how far its front and rear bumpers extend. You will often notice that trucks, buses, and even some cars have vertical rods at the front corners of their vehicles to assist in parking maneuvers.

Leave Parking Spaces Very Carefully

If you pull into a space in a busy parking lot with right-angle parking, your view of the aisle will be blocked by adjoining vehicles. If this is the case, have your passenger stand in the aisle and tell you when it is all clear. If you have no passenger, turn on your flashers and back out very slowly. Collisions in these lots are quite frequent because cars are continuously circulating the aisles and entering and leaving spaces. This includes cars backing out of spaces directly behind you.

Braking

Chapter 2 includes a discussion of perception and reaction times, the two actions that occur immediately prior to your foot hitting the brake. The more alert you are, the more quickly you can hit the brake and bring your car to a halt. The table in Chapter 2 shows that it takes 366 feet or 23 car lengths to stop a car at 60 miles per hour. That exceeds the length of a football field. At 70 miles per hour, the distance is 532 feet. Note that the figures are for a good reaction time, dry pavement and level roadway. The absence of any of those factors will increase the stopping distance even further. It is why the proactive driver is always looking ahead and anticipating what may happen "down the road." And why it is important to begin slowing down immediately if you see danger ahead. So, when you see a potential hazard, take your foot off the accelerator. This slows the vehicle and shortens your reaction time to the brake pedal.

Also look in the rearview mirror at the vehicle behind you when you brake to confirm that the driver following you also slows. Otherwise she may rear-end you. One way to alert her is to tap your brakes slightly before you actually begin to slow down.

Good Brakes, Tires, and Alignment
Poor brakes and bald tires will increase stopping distance just as much as a slippery or downhill road. Poor alignment will cause your car to pull sideways, and even spin sideways if you brake hard.

Antilock Braking System (ABS)
With an antilock braking system, do not pump your brake pedal. Instead, maintain constant downward pressure. The car is not as likely to skid as a car without an ABS, but you may have to do some corrective steering if it does.

No ABS
Push down on the pedal. If you are pressing hard, the vehicle may start to skid. If this happens, let up briefly until the skidding stops and then press it down again. The method for doing this recommended by the American Automobile Association is termed "squeeze braking." In squeeze braking, you put your toes on the brake pedal and place your heel on the floor. Squeeze the pedal down with a steady, firm pressure until just before the brakes lock. If the brakes do lock, relax your toes to release the brake pressure a little. Then, immediately squeeze the brake pedal again to just short of lockup.[5] Also see Chapter 8, "Emergencies."

Wet Brakes

Your brakes will not stop you as fast if they are wet. If this is a concern, press lightly on the brake pedal. Your brakes are probably wet if your car does not slow as quickly as normal. They also may be wet if the car pulls to one side. To dry them, drive slowly and apply light pressure on the brake pedal with your left foot. The friction created often generates enough heat to dry the brakes.[6]

Mountain Roads

Brakes are easily overheated if you use them continuously as you descend a series of steep hills. You can tell if your brakes are overheated by stopping the car and, using your hand, gently reaching between the spokes of the wheel cover and touching the brake disc immediately inside the cover. Overheated brakes mean overheated brake fluid and this can reduce your braking capability. To avoid this, shift down from "drive" (or fourth gear in a manual transmission) to third or second gear and use the engine to slow your descent. If they remain hot, pull to the side of the road until they cool.[7]

Children and Car Seats

The safety of children in a car is of primary concern to parents. For younger kids, this means using correct car seats in the proper fashion. But it is the distractions caused by children that can lead to a crash, whether they are in a car seat or not. For this reason, as well as the safety of the child, the proactive driver will always have their children under control while on the road. And, if this is not working, the driver will pull safely off the road and stop the car until control is regained.

The Law

Passenger restraints include children's car seats as well as adult seat belts. Car seat laws vary from state to state. For example, the law in Virginia requires that all children up to eight years of age must be properly secured in an appropriate car seat or booster seat. Regardless of the law in your state, children are not ready to sit in a vehicle seat using just the lap and shoulder belt until they are at least 4-feet 9-inches tall and weigh 80 pounds.[8]

Providing Proper Safety Seats Is an Ongoing Process

Parents must be aware that the car seat needs of their rapidly growing children are constantly changing. And every time a child is placed in a seat, the parent should check to see that the seat is placed properly and the straps are attached in a safe manner. Each time the family changes cars, the seats will need to be reattached and adjusted. Finally, the various components of the seat should be periodically checked for wear or damage. The importance of careful use cannot be overstated. Over 60 babies strapped into car seats incorrectly are killed every year and another 7,000 are injured.

Infants

Smaller infants up to 20 to 22 pounds should always ride in a rear-facing infant seat or convertible car seat. Larger infants up to 30 to 35 pounds should ride in a rear-facing convertible car seat until they reach at least one year of age, or reach the upper rear-facing weight limit of the seat. Infants should never be placed in the front seat of a vehicle. Nor should they be held in your lap. The forces generated during a crash will put a load on the parent's arms that is twelve times the weight of the child.[9] This will cause the adult to lose their grip of the child.

Toddlers (Children Over One Year and 20 to 40 Pounds)

Children older than one year may ride in a rear-facing convertible car seat until they reach the rear-facing weight limit of the car seat, as long as their head is more than one inch *below* the top of the car seat shell. Children over one year may ride in a forward-facing car seat with a harness if they are over 20 pounds. Premature infants should not be seated facing forward until at least one year after their *due* date, not their birthday. Small and fragile infants and toddlers should remain facing to the rear longer.[10]

Children Who Weigh 40 Pounds or More

Booster seats are used as a transition to vehicle safety belts for children who have outgrown their car seats. However, car seats now available can provide a secure harness system for children up to 80 pounds. This may be a good option for children who are not ready to sit independently in a standard booster seat using a vehicle lap and shoulder belt. Those children over 40 pounds should otherwise use a belt-positioning booster seat until they weigh 80 pounds, are 4-feet 9-inches tall, and can properly use the lap-shoulder belt in a car.[11]

When Buying a Car Seat

Important features of a car seat include a five-point harness rather than a three-point one. "Push-on" style latch connectors are easier to use than hooks. A built-in level indicator and recline adjuster make it easier to insure that the car seat sits at the correct angle. Select simple, easy-to-open chest clips that your baby can't easily move, a simple buckle at the crotch and handle adjusters on the sides that don't require a lot of force. Also look for a simple harness tension adjuster near or below the crotch buckle, and a single-step harness height adjuster that doesn't require you to rethread the straps.[12] Do not buy a second-hand car seat if it has broken or missing parts or if you do not know the seat's history. Only purchase car seats that are approved by the United States Department of Transportation.

When Using a Car Seat

- Never alter your car seat in any way. This includes adding extra padding.
- Take off bulky clothing and coats that prevent your child from being snug in the harness.
- Never take a child out of a safety seat while the car is in motion. Never let them stand up or move around.[13]
- Buckle the car seat in the middle of the back seat if possible.[14]
- In case of a crash, do not remove the child from the car seat until medical personnel check for injuries.

When Is Your Child Big Enough to Use Your Car's Seat Belts?[15]

- The lap portion of the belt fits low across the child's hips, resting on the thighs.
- The shoulder portion fits comfortably across the chest and shoulder, between the neck and the arm, but not on the neck.
- The child is able to sit all the way back in the seat.
- The child's knees bend at the end of the seat cushion.
- The child is able to stay like this for the entire trip.

Further Information

The technology is changing constantly, so be sure to review the current literature before buying your child's car seat. *Consumer Reports* is one source that provides excellent information. One of the very best websites for installation and operation of children's car seats is offered by the Children's Hospital of The King's Daughters Health System in Norfolk, Virginia. The site is www.chkd.org/HealthLibrary/SafetyTips/ChildSafetySeat.aspx.

Quelling Battles

Certain types of wars often start after children are big enough to use normal seat belts. The battle cries include such profound statements as "he looked at me funny" or "she kicked me first." Always pull safely off the road and stop before you attempt to reach behind you and separate the combatants. One way to prevent further conflict may be to suggest that the car will only move when there are no distractions. This takes away the "who's to blame" game.

Conga Lines

Why They Are Dangerous

The Conga was popular in dance halls before most of us were born. Dancers would put their hands on the waist of the dancer in front of them and form a long snake that wove around tables and columns, etc. While this dance craze faded long ago, the expression "conga line" has lived on. On the highway, conga lines form behind slow vehicles, usually on two-lane highways. Examples of slow vehicles include school buses, trucks going uphill, large recreation vehicles, farm equipment or elderly drivers. They are dangerous because they are not traveling at the speed that the overtaking driver expects. If an overtaking driver misjudges their speed and does not slow in time, there will be a rear-end crash. The following paragraphs describe how to pass other cars in a conga line. For more details, see the section of this chapter entitled "Passing."

When to Let Others Pass

As the driver of a slow vehicle, it is important that you warn those behind you by turning on your flashers. Check your rearview mirror frequently to see if there is a line of vehicles behind you. When there are a number of them back there, pull safely over to a legal parking space and let them pass.

Wait Until It Is Safe to Pass

We've harped on the hazard that differences in speed create. Conga lines give a twist to this weighty theory—the difference between actual speed and your desired speed causes a great deal of frustration, so much so that you may act recklessly. Don't! Exercise your highest level of patience and wait for a safe place to pass.

Depending on where you are in the line, you may need to execute several passing maneuvers before you clear the leader. Before you start, check to see that your headlights are on. For each maneuver, put on your left turn signal and pass only as many vehicles as is safe in the length of the passing zone that comes up. And remember to check your rearview mirror before pulling out in case someone behind you is also attempting to pass.

If you are in the conga line and being passed, slow down and provide the passing driver space in front of you in case they have to pull in.

Vehicles Pulling Out in Front of You

Passing more than one vehicle, i.e., the lead vehicle, is inherently dangerous because another vehicle in front of you also may pull out to pass. Watch each vehicle in front of you and its driver for signs that they are going to make a move. Also watch driveways and side streets on the left side of the road for entering vehicles. Finally, look for spaces between the vehicles in the line in front of you in case you suddenly have to pull in. If someone you are passing purposely speeds up, give up the battle and pull in behind. Do not engage in a drag race.

At the Back of the Line

As the last vehicle in a line, flash your brake lights or turn on your flashers if it is legal in your state. Then watch your rearview mirror to be sure that an overtaking driver does not ram you. By leaving a gap between yourself and the vehicle in front of you, you provide yourself enough room to speed up momentarily, should you need to give that rapidly approaching driver additional space.

Courtesy

In the "Introduction" and the section of Chapter 5 entitled, "Attitude," we talked about driver courtesy. You should do at least one act of courtesy each time that your drive! Looking for that opportunity is one very good way for you to keep involved with your driving. Here are a few specific areas of courteous driver actions. Note that the first three are required by law.

1. At a four-way intersection where all four entering roads have a stop sign, the person who arrives first has the go ahead.
2. If two vehicles arrive at the same time at an "uncontrolled intersection (no signal or stop sign.) the one on the right goes first.
3. At night, when a vehicle approaches from the opposite direction, dim your headlights.
4. At night, when a vehicle overtakes you, dim your headlights as soon as they pass.
5. When two lanes of traffic merge, drivers in each lane alternate.
6. When you have just passed a crash or obstruction, you can blink your headlights at oncoming traffic.
7. In some situations, such as when two cars arrive simultaneously at a merge point in a shopping center, the other driver may wave you ahead. Be sure you make eye contact with the driver before doing so. And, *make sure* that the other driver's car is not blocking your view of a third vehicle that is moving into your path.
8. If you are a slow moving vehicle, pull over and let others pass. This is the law in at least one state because of all the visiting recreation vehicles. There you are required to pull over if there are more than five vehicles behind you. Most school bus drivers also are taught to do this (see the preceding section entitled "Conga Lines".)
9. When I stopped in a line at a traffic light, I used to move ahead promptly when it turned green so that those behind me were not delayed. Now, if I'm at the front of the queue, I may wait a few seconds to avoid red-light runners, depending on

the typical habits of the drivers in the state I'm in. But those behind the lead car should still follow promptly.

10. When turning at an intersection, do not wave by an oncoming car that also is turning. The car that was behind you may be passing you on your right.

11. If you are approaching a driveway on your right and a car wishes to turn right out of that driveway into the lane in front of you, you may slow and let the vehicle do so if there is no traffic behind you.

12. Be tolerant of hesitant or confused driving; the driver may be foreign, a beginner, or from out of state. Also be courteous to bicyclists, motorcycles, and trucks.

Recently I was driving in high-speed traffic on I-75 in Georgia and Florida. It was a chance to observe firsthand what one might call "The NASCAR Effect." A surprisingly large percentage of drivers were exhibiting a lack of courtesy as they tailgated and changed lanes without warning, making me believe that they were trying to emulate professional drivers that they had just seen in a NASCAR race. You could actually see other drivers bravely gripping their steering wheels as the reckless speeders threaded through them. This type of discourteous driving works only if the other drivers are aware and are willing to alter their speeds. Crashes at these speeds are disastrous.

There are more courtesy items in the section in Chapter 5 entitled "Right-Of-Way."

Cruise Control

Also known as "speed control," cruise control allows you to set your car at a constant speed. It is usually actuated by a lever on the right side of your steering column. Cruise control should be used sparingly. The reason is that it makes you less alert and attentive. And it will take you an extra instant or two to hit your brakes and take back full control of your car. In crash situations even this briefest of times can be disastrous.

The good news is that advanced forms of speed control are now on the market. These products electronically monitor the distance between your car and the vehicle in front of you. If you get too close, the devices sound an alarm or automatically brake your car.[16] Future versions may offer additional features such as telling you if space is available in an adjoining traffic lane.

Testing Your Cruise Control

You may want to test the sensitivity of your cruise control before you trust it on a busy superhighway. A good place to test it is on a set of closely spaced, steeply rolling hills. Hang on! It may not hold back your speed on steep downhills. Testing it in gusty headwinds will also give you a feel for its capabilities. A good place not to test it is on a curvy road, especially if you are using it for the first time. You do not want a speed control that gives you a jerky ride filled with speed changes. Instead, you want it to modulate your speed in a comfortable way. Most work best on level highways with only gentle curves.

On Interstates
The first and most logical time to use cruise control is when you are on a lightly traveled interstate highway. If you can find one, let me know (there still may be a few!). But even here, you should only use it in the daytime when there is dry pavement. Darkness can hide wildlife and objects on the pavement. And during a skid on wet pavement, the wheels will continue to turn as long as the cruise control remains on.

You can also use cruise control on rural two-lane roads if they do not have sharp curves. But many rural highways (and even some interstates) have sharp curves that require slowing down.

In Small Towns
An interesting use of cruise control is in small towns and villages, places so small that they lack traffic lights and stop signs. There, speed limits may be reduced to 35 miles per hour or less. Most modern cars roll so comfortably that lead-footed drivers find it virtually impossible to hold their cars down to such a slow speed. It is interesting how police situate their radar at the base of a hill entering such a village, a spot where it is doubly hard to keep your car at a low speed. Some drivers believe that this is a good time to use cruise control. I do not. But if you do use cruise control for this purpose, keep your foot poised above the brake and be sure to stay extra alert to conditions ahead. Be especially wary of pedestrians crossing at midblock and vehicles exiting driveways.

When You Shouldn't Use Cruise Control
You should never use your cruise control when it is raining or snowing. If you hydroplane and go off the road, your car will accelerate to the high rate of speed at which you set the speed control. While you have very little control of your car when it hydroplanes, believe me, you are totally in the hands of the gods when your car accelerates on the shoulder.

Debris in the Road

Have you ever come upon debris in your lane? By debris, we mean inanimate objects on an expressway. These might include a piece of tread thrown from a truck tire, a dead animal, a piece of luggage that has fallen off a roof rack, or a plank that slid off the back of a pickup. On most occasions, you will see it in time to safely change lanes or stop. If you don't, and you are traveling at 70 miles per hour, swerving at the last second to avoid the object could flip your car.

It is particularly dangerous if one of your tires goes over a relatively large object as you are swerving. In these instances, it may be better to straddle the object and accept some damage to the bottom of your car. See section of this chapter entitled "Animals on the Road" for a further explanation of this strategy.

Downshifting

You normally operate your car in "Drive" or, if a manual transmission, in the highest forward gear. You can "downshift" to a lower gear to provide more power for climbing a steep hill. You also may downshift to slow your vehicle on downhills. On severe downhills, downshifting is necessary to avoid overheating your brakes. When overheated, brakes can fail. A rule of thumb advanced by motorists towing trailers is to downshift to the same gear that you needed to climb the hill. Downshifting also will give you more traction on a wet or icy road. Also see the section of this chapter entitled "Uphills."

Driving on the Left

We have always driven on the right in the United States. In 1792, Pennsylvania legislators were the first to pass a law mandating the practice.[17] However, our first cars were manufactured with the steering wheel in the middle or on the right. That was until 1910, when Lee Frayer of the Firestone-Columbus (Ohio) Motor Company moved the steering wheel to the left side. The reason? Lee thought that it was safer for the driver to sit on the left side where he could more accurately judge the lateral distance between his car and an oncoming vehicle.[18] It was not so that his right arm would be free to hug his lady love.

There are many places around the world where you must drive on the left. Autos that are sold in Australia, Bermuda, Britain, Hong Kong, India, Ireland, Kenya, New Zealand, Pakistan, Scotland, Singapore, and South Africa have their steering wheel on the right. In Britain, the practice dates back to the days when bandits roamed the English countryside. Men wore swords to defend themselves. Since most men were right handed, the sword was put into use on the right side of their horse. In the interest of instant readiness, they kept their horse to the left when they encountered oncoming riders. That explains why people in England (and places influenced by England) still drive on the left.[19] Quaint, isn't it?

If you do drive in these countries, do not practice here in the states before your trip. And, ask a passenger (if you have one) to repeat "left, left, left!" as you approach each roundabout and intersection. Also, be prepared for some outbursts of advice and profanity from any passengers. It is disconcerting to ride in the front left seat in these places. Much like the character in the movie "Dr. Strangelove," we keep reaching for a steering wheel that is not there. And without the security of its presence in front of us we get the heebie-jeebies.

On my last trip to Scotland, I picked up a rental car near the railroad station in Edinburgh. Within the first quarter mile I had committed some great sin that caused a car of teenagers to yell and toot at me. I think it was something "minor" like going around a traffic circle in the wrong direction.

Once out in the countryside, things were much easier. Or they were until I made a left turn into the wrong lane and came radiator to radiator with a very sympathetic farm couple. My two passengers were screaming at me. And while there was no collision, I was thoroughly shaken. So, it may be well to avoid driving a car in these countries, especially if you are older. If you do drive, try to start in a rural area and please be careful and patient. Also, pay extra, if necessary, to rent a car with an automatic transmission. This helps tremendously when you are going through narrow streets and small villages.

Drunk Driving

Various states refer to drunk driving as driving while intoxicated (DWI), driving under the influence (DUI), or operating under the influence (OUI). Approximately one million people are injured annually and fifteen thousand are killed because of drunk drivers. Three out of every five Americans will be involved in an alcohol-related crash at some time in their lives. The majority of impaired drivers killed are highly intoxicated and over half are repeat offenders.[20] Proactive drivers never operate their cars while under the influence of alcohol or drugs; those who may take a few drinks have prearranged with a companion to take away their keys. The more difficult issue is dealing with another car that is piloted by a drunk. That's where scouting ahead and being able to read other drivers becomes extremely important (see Chapter 3).

The Tipsy Twins

One summer day shortly after my twelfth birthday, I overheard my parents laughing uncontrollably about a drunken driving incident in our rural community. It involved two brothers who would drive their old farm truck a mile up the hill to the local bar after getting their milk check in the mail. Or, more precisely, about their subsequent trip home. At three in the afternoon on a sunny summer day, these two completely inebriated dairymen boarded their battered pickup and started down the hill. Their eyes were so dulled by alcohol that they thought it was raining. Thus, their truck wandered back and forth across the road with its wipers going. Suddenly, the driver imagined that he heard a loud noise. He pulled to the side of the road and stopped. Then he insisted that his brother get out and inspect the vehicle.

The passenger side door opened and the driver's brother sprawled headlong into a deep ditch. Recovering himself, he moved around the truck where his eyes fixated on the bald left rear tire. He then put his head between the tire and the fender in order to eyeball the tread up close. At that moment, two kids rode by on bikes. Seeing them, the driver called to his brother that two heifers were loose and that the brothers best hurry back to the farm. The driver then engaged the clutch and caught his brother's head between the tire and the fender. Fortunately, one of the young cyclists quickly sized up the situation and shouted "Whoa!" at the top of his lungs. The driver stopped.

A neighbor who had been watching ran out to the truck, pulled the driver onto the street, sat him down and admonished him in a most forceful manner. Meanwhile, the neighbor's wife called the local garage. The garage's tow truck appeared within minutes. The driver used the truck's hoist to lift the bed of the pickup. This dislodged the head of the rapidly sobering brother. At the time, I could see the humor, but it did make drunk driving appear dangerous. In today's world, such a story is not the least bit humorous.

The Near Misses

Just three days later, an event turned my ambivalence into a lifetime fear of drunk drivers. That day I almost lost my life. I was riding my bike to a friend's house around one o'clock in the afternoon. It was sunny and the road was dry. As I approached a very sharp curve, a speeding car came around the turn toward me. Its tires screeched and then the inside tires lifted into the air. The driver over-steered to the inside of the curve and then spun the wheel the other way. That rolled the car over onto its left side. It slid towards me on its side. As it came, there were terrible sounds of tearing metal. Above that rose the horrified screams of the two women in the back seat. The crumpled car stopped 25 feet away. And that is when I started shaking uncontrollably. Later I learned that the people inside the car had been drinking at a local bar. Fortunately none of them died (for a more deadly example, see the Foreword).

Our Lenient Laws

There is a strong feeling that the laws against drunk driving are much too lenient. In many states a first offense brings only probation; no jail, no fine, no restricted driver's license, no community service, no mandatory attendance at Alcoholics Anonymous meetings. It is only for the third offense that actual jail time is meted out, and this can be served on weekends. By that time, some of these drunks have killed or maimed someone. They seldom kill or maim themselves.

Fortunately, some states are adopting much stricter laws. Maine has a zero-tolerance law for drivers under 21, with a 12- to 18-month license suspension for any measurable amount of alcohol in their blood (blood alcohol content greater than 0.0). For those over 21, a first offense carries a 90-day license suspension and a $400.00 fine, while a fourth offense can carry a six-year license suspension, seven months in jail, and a $2,400.00 fine. A conviction for vehicular homicide can result in a prison term of up to 30 years and a permanent loss of license.[21]

Drunken drivers may be in for another surprise. A conviction could cost them as much as $7,000.00. Here is the tabulation that one finds posted on the walls of restrooms in many Maine bars:[22]

Towing Charges	$50.00
Bail Bond	$25.00
Lawyer	$2,000.00
Fine	$500.00
Alcohol Education Course	$105.00
3-Year Insurance Surcharge	$4,000.00
Loss of Work Time	$300.00
Total	$6,980.00

Table 4: Estimated cost of drunk-driving arrest in Maine

It is interesting that in Sweden a first offense is one year in jail with no time off for good behavior. A second offense is punishable by a three-year jail sentence.[23] That sounds like an even better idea.

TECHNOLOGY

The National Highway Traffic Safety Administration and others are developing and testing technology that will keep drunk drivers off the road. It is a long-term research project and involves ways of unobtrusively and accurately measuring whether the driver's blood alcohol level is over the legal limit. The objective is to prevent a drunk driver from starting the car.[24]

MARIJUANA

Special DUI laws regarding marijuana are under development as states legalize the use of this substance for medicinal purposes.

Dust Storms

Dust storms occur mostly in southwestern states. In Arizona, dust storms happen most frequently between May and September, especially along sections of Interstates I-8 and 10. They are unpredictable and occur when high winds blow across unplanted agricultural fields or dry desert terrain. This causes dust to engulf nearby highways for brief periods.

Motorists that see a dust storm coming or are engulfed in one should pull a safe distance off the road and wait for it to pass. They should turn off their lights, set their emergency brake and makes sure that their regular brake light is off. If they can't pull off the road immediately, they should proceed at a reduced speed using the centerline as a guide until they find a safe place to leave the roadway. They should never stop on the pavement.[25]

Energy-Saving Strategies

The most effective energy-saving strategy is to buy a more fuel-efficient car. How much can this save? Let's say you drive your car twelve thousand miles per year. Going from a car that gets 15 miles per gallon to one that gets 30 miles per gallon saves $1,200.00 a year at $3.00 per gallon and $1,600.00 at $4.00 per gallon.

Smaller Cars

The more fuel-efficient car is usually smaller and lighter and does not come out as well in collisions with its bigger cousins. However, crashworthiness of smaller cars is vastly improved today and there will probably be fewer big cousins in the future. And more fuel-efficient vehicles often are cheaper than those big cousins. Currently, the Ford Fusion Hybrid is rated at an average of almost 40 miles per gallon for city and highway travel.[26] In the previous example, that would produce an annual savings of $1,500 if gas is $3 per gallon.

Optimum Engine Speed

If you can't afford to buy a new car, there are a number of other strategies available. The first is to drive your car at its optimum engine speed for fuel consumption. This is usually 55 miles per hour unless your car has an unusually sleek aerodynamic shape. Just speeding up to 60 mile per hour can cut your fuel efficiency by seven to eight percent.

If your car has a tachometer, you can also keep the engine turning at or near its optimum speed (revolutions per minute). The optimum engine speed for fuel efficiency is not currently shown on the new vehicle window sticker but it should be. Ask your dealer for the information. And remember, going an optimum speed of 55 miles per hour is obviously not a good idea on a freeway with a 75–miles-per-hour speed limit or in a school zone with a 25–miles-per-hour speed limit.

Avoid Start-and-Stop Driving

Even if you can't always drive at optimum engine speed, you can still save considerable fuel by not tailgating and by not accelerating and braking rapidly. Sure, you understand the thing about not accelerating rapidly, but what is so bad about hard braking? It's really very simple. You stop sooner so you have to begin using your engine sooner to move forward. One writer claims that the jerkiest of jerky city drivers may be able to reduce gas consumption by a whopping 33 per cent if they drive at a constant speed![27]

Extended Idling

It is usually better to stop and restart your car if you will be waiting for over a minute. A typical vehicle uses a cup of gas every six minutes that it idles.[28]

Close Windows at High Speeds

Open windows allow air to enter the car and create added wind resistance. The extra work that results for your engine will use more fuel. At high speeds, it is more economical to close your windows and operate the air conditioner.[29]

Aerodynamic Design

The profile of your car is aerodynamically designed to maximize mileage. You can take best advantage of this by not putting stuff on the roof of your car.

Engine Maintenance

Other strategies include replacing dirty air filters and keeping your motor properly tuned. Experts claim fuel savings of approximately 10 percent.

Tire Inflation

One strategy that is of particular interest has to do with your tires. Experts report that going from improperly to properly inflated tires can increase your mileage 10 percent. That would save $220.00 to $290.00 per year in fuel costs in the example that we gave at the beginning of this section. Proper levels of tire inflation for your car are listed on your car door and in your owner's manual. Using standard radial tires also increases gas mileage.

You could save more by choosing specialized radial tires that have more fuel-efficient treads. But this may not be a good tradeoff because you sacrifice the tire traction that you need for safe turning, good braking, and a better grip on wet or icy highways. Tire makers are scrambling to help you, though, so keep reading the literature and decide for yourself.

Car Pooling and Combining Trips

Car pooling and combining trips are two very good ways to save fuel.

Interactive Technology

Automakers are beginning to introduce new cars with technology that encourages a more efficient driving style. Research indicates that these electronic prompts can make a significant dent in fuel consumption. The options run the gamut from simple displays of fuel consumption, to interactive video games, to a gas pedal that actually pushes back when you stomp on it. Most of these technologies can be ignored or turned off if the driver wishes.[30]

No-Nos

Here are a few things that you should *not* do. The first is to turn the engine off and coast. This can cause the car to lose its braking and steering assist. Worse, the steering wheel can lock. At this point, you completely lose control of your car.

Another technique being bandied about is to draft (or tuck in tightly behind) tractor-trailers just like bike racers draft other cyclists. Rest assured, you will be toast if the truck driver suddenly stops. You have neither the time nor the space to brake safely.

Perhaps the most outrageous of the fuel saving hints is to roll through stop signs. You will be lucky if all you get is a ticket. You may already have a friend who became a quadriplegic because he rolled a stop sign. I do.

Farm Machinery

The idiosyncrasies of farm machinery are not well known to urban and suburban drivers. The most important is their very slow speed. Farm equipment speeds of 15 miles per hour will cause your car to rear-end them if you don't slow immediately. This may require you to slam on your brakes if you come over a hill on a country road and see farm machinery immediately in front of you.

Another difficulty is passing farm machinery. Well-meaning farmers perched high on a tractor seat often can see further ahead than you and will wave you around if they think that the coast is clear. Since you are placing your life in their hands, I would suggest that you eyeball the farmer carefully before pulling out. Here's a few other items that you should know about farm tractors and their tows:[31]

- Farm machinery is often wider than cars and trucks and can occupy a lane and a half of rural highway.
- Machinery half on the road and half on the shoulder may suddenly move completely onto the road.
- Farm machinery operators may not be able to see you due to the large equipment they are towing. If you can't see the operator, they can't see you. And their equipment may not have rearview mirrors.
- Farm machinery is not required to have brake lights or turn signals.
- Farm machinery crossing from one side of the road to the other may be pulling equipment that will take longer to clear the highway.
- Farm machinery that is slowing down or pulling toward the right side of the road may be preparing for a wide turn to the left. These types of turns are the biggest single cause of all farm-related deaths because following motorists are impatient or unaware of the need for the equipment to make a wide turn.

Many of these same rules apply to construction machinery. However, construction machinery is usually protected by advance warning signs, flashing lights, and flaggers.

Fog

Turn on your headlights when driving in fog (actually, they should be on all the time). As with snowstorms, low beams often work better than high beams. The low beams point down and their light does not bounce off the fog particles or snowflakes and reflect back into your eyes. If you drive in fog frequently, you may opt to install fog lights as well. If you do, remember to leave them off during normal conditions or when meeting other drivers as they can blind the operator of an oncoming car. Also, remember to turn on your wipers. This is easy to forget in a fine fog or mist when you don't notice that your visibility is gradually diminishing.

And please don't ever drive in dense fog. You have to go very slowly to avoid outrunning the distance that you can see ahead. If you drive that slowly, there is the possibility of someone coming up behind you at an unsafe speed and rear-ending you. If you are suddenly caught in fog, you might try to catch a "seeing eye" driver that is traveling at a slightly faster speed ahead of you and stay a safe distance behind him. At best, that is a temporary fix. You should get well off the road as soon as you can and turn out your lights (see the discussion of whiteouts in Chapter 7).

Fog Lights
See the sections of this chapter entitled "Fog" and "Headlights."

Freeway Driving and Interchanges

Freeways are multi-lane, divided roads designed for high-speed travel. They also may be known as expressways, interstates, throughways, turnpikes, or toll roads, although the last two are not free. Freeway driving is actually a series of very different maneuvers involving entrance and exit ramps as well as the freeway itself. Of these, negotiating the weaving section at an interchange is often the most difficult.

Entrance Ramps
Accelerate close to freeway speed as you come to the end of an entrance ramp. Since differences in speed are dangerous, it is best to reach a speed that is close to that of the traffic on the freeway before entering the freeway travel lane. Of course, some freeways do not have long enough ramps to do this. Particularly tight ramps may even have a stop sign at their junction with the freeway.

Ramp Metering
In some urban areas such as Portland, Oregon, each entrance ramp is equipped with traffic signals near the end as they converge on the freeway. These signals may be red when you arrive, but will turn green as traffic on the freeway thins. Their purpose is to reduce

freeway congestion by spacing out the entering vehicles. Gates also may be used. Persons first encountering these gates will see gaps on the freeway and wonder why the gate is closed. It is because a certain number of gaps are required to keep the traffic flowing downstream where more vehicles are entering.

Merging Onto the Freeway

If you are accelerating to a higher speed you should be aware of the traffic in the lane that you are going to enter. You can usually get a general idea of traffic conditions on the freeway by looking as you approach the on-ramps. As you come down the ramp, use your side-view mirror to spot a gap. Increase or decrease your speed to fit into this gap as you merge onto the freeway. Remember, you will be driving faster than you did on the local streets.

Of special interest during your entrance to the freeway is how you operate your turn signal. First, signal for your turn onto the entrance ramp. This is usually a right turn. Once on the ramp, flip the signal lever to the left to signal to freeway traffic that you are merging from the ramp into the right lane of the freeway. Never cut across freeway lanes as you enter the freeway. It is unexpected and dangerous. Instead, stay in the right lane until you adjust your speed for flow conditions such as heavy traffic or a large number of trucks.

On the Freeway

Once on the freeway, drive at a speed that is consistent with the other cars, preferably at or close to the speed limit. Again, this is the safest because it minimizes the differences in speed among vehicles. Some vehicles will be going faster than you, and some, slower. You are traveling at about the average speed if you pass the same number of vehicles as pass you. However, there will be some conditions, such as fog or ice, where you will want to go slower or even exit the freeway.

Normally, the right-hand lane should be your home. On a three-lane freeway, the right lane might be designated for trucks. In that case, you might select the center lane. On some roads, the right lane has been worn and is filled with potholes so the left lane may be a better choice in light traffic. If you do drive in the left lane, watch your rearview mirror and move back to the right lane if you are being overtaken by another vehicle.

Courteous drivers will move to the left lane when they see a vehicle descending an entry ramp onto the right lane. The courteous driver then expects the entering driver to stay in the right lane initially, thus avoiding competition for space with their car.

Be sure to check your mirror before changing lanes. On busier freeways, a slug of cars coming down a ramp can produce backups. That is one of the reasons why cities like Portland use ramp metering.

A frequent crash on freeways occurs when an exiting vehicle is rear-ended. This happens when that vehicle decelerates unexpectedly while still on the freeway. To avoid this possibility, activate your turn signal before exiting. If the exit ramp is long enough, use the ramp for most of your deceleration.

You do not want to be stuck on a freeway when driving conditions deteriorate. Weather may render the freeway completely unusable. Fog and whiteouts, for example, can occur suddenly. Do not assume that other drivers will slow down. Even with continuous fog, drivers tend to go so fast that they cannot see a hazard in time to brake safely. In ice or snow, a safe road can instantly turn into a sheet of ice. Heavy rain can blind a driver. A blizzard can trap you in a snow bank.

Knowing how much gas you have and other factors that may require you to leave the freeway is important so that you do not become stranded. Exit signs usually state the distance to the next exit. They often state the distance to the next gas station as well. Be prepared to get off the road and stay overnight at a motel or use local roads, no matter how much longer it takes. You may avoid a crash or being trapped in a snow bank.

Interchanges and Weaving Sections

Freeway interchanges are normally either a full or partial cloverleaf. The full cloverleaf is more expensive to build and is most often found where two freeway cross. A partial interchange is usually built when a freeway crosses a local street. More discussion about entrance and exit ramps for partial interchanges appears earlier in this section.

The advantage of a full cloverleaf is that it does not require any left turns on either highway. However, the full cloverleaf can create a potentially dangerous weaving section where traffic leaving the freeway must merge with entering cars. There are two types of weaving sections. The better type has a barrier between the freeway and the weaving lane. The more dangerous type lacks a separation of the weaving lane from through traffic. Some of these latter weaving sections are quite short, requiring the leaving driver to merge with the entering car and then immediately weave right onto the exit ramp. Those entering the freeway must crane their neck back to the left to check for exiting traffic, merge with that traffic, and then accelerate onto the freeway.

Weaving sections should be navigated with *extreme care*. It is very difficult for the entering vehicle to match the high speed of the cars exiting the freeway if you are entering on a sharply curved ramp. There are many simultaneous decisions that you must make in a short time as you locate a gap in the existing vehicles on the freeway. These include choosing the correct speed, timing your entry, activating your turn signals, locating a gap, crossing the exiting vehicles, and merging with the main stream of traffic. Typically, both drivers will adjust their speeds to provide space in front of or behind them for the other driver as they execute this maneuver.

Gas and Gas Stations

No one likes to walk several miles to get a gallon of gas when the tank runs dry. That is why experts suggest that you fill up before your tank gets down to a quarter full. This is particularly important if you anticipate being caught in a traffic delay during your trip. Maintenance experts also note that continuously operating your car with a low fuel level will damage your fuel pump.[32]

It is easy to agonize over the price of gas these days. I know an individual from Queens, New York, who was convinced that the cheapest gas was in Hoboken, New Jersey. He was so sure of this that as soon as his tank was half full, he drove through Brooklyn, across Lower Manhattan, and into the Holland Tunnel just to reach his favorite filling station. Trouble is, by the time he got home, the cost of the extra gas that he had to use probably offset the money that he saved.

In a Hurry?
If so, see which of your neighborhood gas stations has the fastest pumps. The fastest can pump a gallon in about three seconds.

Pumping Protocol
Some people like to set the clip on the nozzle that keeps it open when they fuel. Others may stick their gas cap in the pump handle to hold it open. If you do, you still must be vigilant. A sign at my local gas station says it all: "A Person Shall Remain In Attendance Outside Of The Vehicle And In View Of The Nozzle." In New Jersey and Oregon, your fuel must be pumped for you by gas station employees.

Miles per Gallon
To compute your gas mileage, fill your tank and write down your odometer reading. Then, when your tank gets low, fill it up again and note the odometer reading. The difference in mileage between the two represents the distance that you have traveled since your previous fill. If you have a trip odometer, you can reset it to "0" when you fill the tank and avoid the mileage calculation. Either way, divide the mileage by the gallons that you added at the second fill and you have the miles per gallon for your car. Compare your miles per gallon for city driving to those for freeway driving. The numbers will allow you to budget your gas money. They may even help you decide if you need a more fuel-efficient vehicle.

Gas Tank Capacity
The fuel gauge on some cars is extremely conservative. For these vehicles, the low gas indicator light comes on well ahead of an empty tank. To check out the actual reserve, drive your car until that light comes on. As soon as possible, fill the tank. Now compare the number of gallons that you put in to the capacity of the tank that is shown in your Owner's Manual. Let's say that the difference is 3 gallons. If you calculated that your car gets 20 miles per gallon, then you can go 60 miles before you actually run out of gas. This can become especially important if you have to travel in an area where there are few gas stations.

Grade of Gas

Consult your owner's manual. If it says to use regular gas, then using premium gas will be a waste of money. On the other hand, if it says that your car requires premium gas, then that is what you should use. Recently, however, the lawyers have put equivocal language in some of the manuals. For these cars, the current advice is to calculate your mileage using each of the different grades of gasoline. If the miles per gallon figures are nearly the same, you save money if you use regular gas. If the difference is two miles per gallon or more, you may actually save money using the more expensive fuel. And, you will keep the get-up-and-go that your engine is designed to provide. That gives you an extra margin of safety if you need to accelerate quickly.[33]

Water and Dirt in Gas Station Tanks

One thing to be wary of when you are in a gas station is the gas company's huge delivery truck. If its driver is filling the storage tanks, it may be better for you to go to another station or come back later. It seems that some water and dirt harmlessly accumulate in these tanks. However, when the storage tank is being filled, the water and dirt mixes with the gas, the sediment gets stirred up and can then find its way into your fuel tank. It is better to wait until the tanks have sat a while after being filled.

Defective Pump Shutoff

We are conditioned to have the gas pump shut off automatically when our tank is full. Just recently, I used a gas pump with a defective pump shutoff. All of a sudden there was gas all over my car, my trousers, my shoes, and the ground. Not only is this stinky and messy, it is dangerous. The giveaway is when you first remove the nozzle to start pumping. If the hose is already full of gas, put it back and go to another pump.

No-Name Gas Stations

Independent gas stations usually buy their fuel from larger, name-brand oil companies, so it's not much different from what you get for a higher price at a name-brand station. Sometimes it's formulated without additives designed to clean your engine, but *Consumer Reports* advises that your car should run fine on that gas.[34]

The Myth of Denser Gas

A common tip is to buy gas in the morning, when the air is cool. The theory is that the cooler gasoline will be denser, so you will get more for your money. However, the temperature of the gas changes very little, if at all, because most gas is stored underground.[35]

Also see the section of this chapter entitled "Energy-Saving Strategies."

Headlights

More and more cars are being sold with either the parking lights or the headlights set to be permanently on when the engine is running. Others automatically turn on at dusk. These are important and proven safety features. If your car is not so equipped, make sure you have one or the other on at all times. As more and more drivers travel with their headlights always on, they are less likely to see a car whose headlights are off during the day. Today, over 60 percent of the autos on the road operate with their headlights on at all times.[36]

Also know if your car has an automatic cutoff for the lights when you turn off the ignition. If not, and you forget to turn off your lights, you may end up with a dead battery. Here are some recommendations:

- Run your car with the headlights on at all times.
- If you insist on having them off during the day, turn them on at least twenty minutes before sunset and after dark. Also turn them on if the day is overcast.
- Turn your headlights on whenever your windshield wipers are on.
- Use low beams when there is a constant stream of oncoming cars.
- Dim your lights before your beams are pointed directly toward a solitary oncoming car.; i.e., when you first see its lights approaching from over a hill or around a bend. About 1,000 feet is a good distance.
- Also dim them when you are within 500 feet of a car that you are overtaking. Even your low beams can reflect off the rearview mirror and blind the driver in front of you if you tailgate.
- Use low beams in snow and fog.
- Don't out-drive your headlights. Reduce your speed to match the distance that you can see ahead. High beams typically reach out 350 feet and low beams, 160 feet.[37]
- Dim your headlights to alert other motorists to emergencies.
- Keep a soft cloth in your car and clean your headlights before driving. You also may have to stop and clean your headlights in icy conditions.

As mentioned in the section of this chapter entitled "Fog," you may wish to install fog lights on your car. These lights are usually mounted beneath the regular headlights with their beams directed downward. Use them for fog and snow. But turn them off during normal nighttime conditions when another car is coming towards you. Otherwise the combination of the fog lights and your normal headlights may blind the oncoming driver.

Hitchhikers

No!

Horns

One of the most dangerous things you can do is rely solely on your horn to prevent a crash. What are you saying by leaning on your horn? That continuous blast states that you feel that you are entitled to the space in the road ahead that the other vehicle (or person) is soon going to occupy. It is the worst possible collision-avoidance strategy. You are relying on someone who is unaware of what they are doing to stop or change their direction of travel.

You must use your horn to alert the other party but, at the same instant, *also* take your own immediate corrective action such as braking or turning away from the impending crash. If you just blow your horn, you lose valuable reaction and braking time. The lost time may make the difference between a serious crash and no crash at all. And, the other driver may not hear your horn. The typical state legal requirement is that horns be heard from up to 200 feet away. This may not be enough distance at freeway speeds. Remember that the horn's purpose is as a warning or alert to potential hazard, not an instrument of venting—don't resort to using it in anger or impatience.

Leaning hard on your horn *is* very important in certain emergency situations. One is if you are having a medical emergency such as a heart attack. Another is to alert other drivers if your brakes fail (see Chapter 8, "Emergencies"). The third would be if you are threatened by a criminal or road rager. If you hear another car's blaring horn, be alert to these possibilities.

Hydroplaning

During a rainstorm, a thin coat of oil rises to the surface of the pavement. This film can float away in several minutes or it may remain as long as a half hour. Flooding or melting snow may create a layer of water on top of the pavement. A layer of water also forms during a rain storm if the highway is rutted, which often happens to heavily used asphalt roads. Another instance is during a winter warming spell on a highway that shows a set of tire tracks in each direction but is otherwise covered with snow.

All of the above situations can cause hydroplaning. When your car hydroplanes, it will feel like it is floating and will continue in its original direction no matter which way you turn the wheels. To regain traction, you must slow down. That is why it is good to slow down anyway when there is precipitation. One source suggests a 33 percent reduction in speed in rain and a 50 percent reduction in speed in snow. If there is a car ahead of you, it may be helpful to follow along in their tire tracks.[38]

Intersections

Unlike freeway interchanges, intersections are entirely at ground level. With the growth in urban and suburban traffic, negotiating intersections of multi-lane highways is becoming one of the most common and dangerous driving experiences. In fact, it is reported that over 80 percent of all city crashes occur within signalized intersections.[39] This is a good time to recall that the first step in proactive driving is scouting the route ahead.

Who Has the Right-Of-Way?

The Uniform Vehicle Code advises that when two vehicles come to an intersection at the same time, the one on the right has the right-of-way.[40] This rule was first created by a French professor of physics in 1896. It was directed at bicycle riders.

As early as 1922, people were proposing to give the person on the left the right-of-way.[41] This is the rule for today's roundabouts and traffic circles. The rule gives the right-of-way to traffic already in the roundabout. Without the left-hand rule, the roundabout would fill with traffic and come to a halt. It's interesting to note that Roman Chariot races and today's NASCAR races also operate in a counterclockwise direction. Additional discussions of right-of-way issues can be found in the "Right-Of-Way" section of Chapter 5 and the "Roundabouts" section in this chapter.

Confused? You are not alone.

Mega Intersections

In recent years we have seen the arrival of the mega intersection. These are a less expensive solution than constructing overpasses, particularly in very flat states such as Florida. A typical mega intersection might have 20 lanes of traffic feeding into it. In other words, there would be five lanes on each of the approach legs. This typically includes three through lanes, a left turn lane and a right turn lane.

Arrive in the Correct Lane

It is important to apply the three-step process of looking ahead, determining the correct lane, and moving into it when you approach a mega intersection. The more complex the intersection, the more important this is. Picking the correct lane is easier to do if you pass through the intersection on a daily basis. However, as a newcomer, you may find yourself in the wrong lane. If you are, do not suddenly cut across two lanes to make a left-hand turn. Instead of surprising the drivers in the adjoining lanes, continue on to the next intersection and turn left there. If traffic is extremely heavy and you are on a grid system, it may even be better to make three right turns to achieve your left turn!

Jug Handles

Many years ago, the State of New Jersey improved traffic flow and driver safety by making it possible to turn left from the right lane. As you exit to the right into the "jug handle," you loop around to your left. The jug handle ends with your car at a traffic light facing the street that you are seeking. As the light for the traffic on the freeway that you just exited turns red, you get a green light and can cross without the danger of oncoming vehicles.

Stop Lines

Intersections are discussed more extensively in the sections in this chapter entitled "Stop Signs" and "Traffic Lights." Common to both of these are stop lines. Do you roll past these lines before you stop? The lines are placed so that your car is not in the path of a vehicle turning in front of you from your right. Because of this, it is often a good idea to stop several feet behind the line.

Also see the section of this chapter entitled "Stop Signs" to understand why it is so important to come to a complete stop. For a different type of intersection, read the section of this chapter entitled "Roundabouts."

Jake Brakes

What are Jake Brakes? They are engine brakes that truckers use to slow down their vehicles. The noise from an unexpected application by a huge rig just as you are passing can scare you into the ditch (I hope not). To apply them, the trucker flips a switch on his dashboard. This restricts the engine exhaust when he lets up on his fuel pedal. The backup of the exhaust slows the truck and causes a huge amount of noise. In Colorado, trucks are required by law to have mufflers for engine brakes. And some communities in other states prohibit their use during all or part of the day. For example, signs in Pittsburgh, Pennsylvania, read "No Engine Braking Within City Limits." Be prepared for their noise when you are passing trucks.

Leaving the Car

- Make sure you select a legal parking space.
- If you park on a hill, turn the wheels into the curb and set the emergency brake.
- Is your car one of the few whose headlights remain on when you shut off the ignition? If so, turn those lights off!
- Always lock the car, but make sure you have the keys before you do. In fact, carry two sets of keys. It is *very* expensive to get into today's cars without a key! If there are two people involved, each should have a set of keys. You may need to go to a dealer with your vehicle identification number if you lose your keys. Hiding keys under the vehicle is an alternative, but thieves can easily locate these.

- Do not leave valuables in the car. If something valuable must be left in the car, leave it out of sight.
- In high-crime neighborhoods, consider using an antitheft device such as a club or an alarm.
- Also consider an antitheft device if your car is a popular model for thieves. Watch your local paper for its top ten list of "thievable" cars.
- Remember where you leave your car. Write down the location if it's a huge parking lot. Specialty catalogues also offer pocket-sized GPS-based locators.
- Do not leave children unattended in the car.
- Roll down a window slightly if you leave a pet inside. In hot or especially cold weather, take the pet with you.
- In hot weather, consider putting a sunshade in the window.

At this point, we'll mention "Mad Passenger Disease" a malady in which the occupant of the right front seat attempts to leave the car before it is stopped. Not a wise idea, although perhaps not as serious as "Mad Driver's Disease" in which the driver starts off before the passengers have completely boarded. Also see the section of this chapter entitled "Drunk Driving."

Looking Out for Other Cars

Recall that you as a proactive driver are continuously scanning the road ahead and to the side. This scanning should locate other traffic that you will encounter. There are other ways to look for traffic as well:

- At a stop sign, look left and right twice before entering the main highway. Conventional wisdom has you looking once to the left (oncoming traffic), once to the right, and then again to the left. You should look both ways *twice* to pick up anything such as a motorcycle or a white car in winter that you missed with your first glance. This is especially important if you have a vision problem such as glaucoma that enlarges your blind spot. Also see the section of this chapter entitled "Stop Signs."
- Before you pull out to pass, you should turn your head to the left and look both to your left and behind you. A trick here is to remember to turn both your neck and torso. By turning both you can look directly behind you.
- A special situation is when a car is coming toward your street from a side road or entrance ramp. For this situation, see the section entitled "Stop Signs."

- If in a populated area, watch the parked cars as well. If you see a person sitting in the driver's seat, the car may be about to move. Also watch for pedestrians popping out from between the parked cars.

Math and Physics

Car Coming at You

Driving technique is all about math and physics. For example, your brain immediately starts estimating the speed of an oncoming car on a two-lane road as it crosses into your lane in order to passes another vehicle. You are deciding if you have to pull onto the shoulder to get out of its way. Your brain is doing a lot of math in arriving at this decision, as it calculates velocities and determines the time that you will meet head-on if he doesn't pull back into his lane. See Chapter 8, "Emergencies," for actions that you can take in this situation.

Curves

When you round a sharp curve, you feel yourself being pushed to the outside by centrifugal force. That is physics, pure and simple. On wet pavement, you develop a feel for what speed is uncomfortable for you and what speed will cause your tires to lose their grip on the road and make your car skid off the curve. Learning to keep math and physics on your mind as you drive can alert you more quickly to other dangerous situations as well.

Narrow Lanes

Do you know how long and wide your car is? For instance, a minivan might be 17 feet long and 6½ feet wide. How about the width of a freeway lane? A modern freeway lane is 12 feet wide. This means that if you are in the middle of your lane, there is almost three feet of clear pavement on either side of you. If you are on a four-lane freeway, and the driver of an adjacent car is centered in her lane opposite you, your vehicles will be 5½ feet apart. That is a very safe distance. Now, imagine you are at a place where the road narrows during a bridge repair. The lane width may be as little as 10 feet. And, say there is a tractor-trailer in the lane next to you. Tractor-trailers can be as much as nine feet across. Now you and the tractor-trailer are less than three feet apart! This deserves a lot more of your attention as a driver. Consider slowing down to avoid having a truck adjacent to you when you pass through such a restrictive bottleneck. Also see the section of this chapter entitled "Wide Loads."

Car Selection

You may also use math and physics to help select a car. One car that I've driven for years is a Subaru. The car has a stability control system and a horizontally opposed engine that gives it a lower center of gravity. To my mind, this type of design means superior driving performance.[42] And there is probably less chance of a rollover.

Motorcycles

Unlike ATVs, motorcycles are designed to operate on public highways. And they are more likely to have an experienced driver at their helm. The problem for us motorists is that we are not looking for them when we leave our driveway or turn onto a road. That is why we suggest that you look twice in both directions before turning. Even if you don't actually see the bike with your first glance, your second peek will tell you that something has moved since you first looked.

Mud Season

The moisture in dirt roads in colder regions of the United States will freeze solid during the winter. But in the spring, the temperatures rise and the roads can turn to oozing mud. What first occurs is the "pudding" phase, in which only the first few inches of frost leave. It is particularly treacherous because immediately below is a smooth layer of ice. As the thaw continues, the mud can become as much as a foot or more deep. In this situation, it is important to keep your car moving so that you don't get stuck. Ruts created by previous drivers can prove challenging as you attempt to keep the wheel straight and maintain momentum.

Whatever the condition, caution and reduced speed at high revs are the order of the day when driving on these roads in mud season. A visit to a car wash afterwards would probably be indicated if you wish to tell which car is yours in the supermarket parking lot. Perhaps the most notorious of mud seasons occurs in Vermont where many roads are unpaved and the winter temperatures are quite low. Mud season there often lasts from March to May.

Parking

There are two types of parking spaces: parallel and head-in. Head-in parking includes right-angle parking and any angle in between.

Parallel Parking
Parallel parking is found along many city streets. The ability to parallel park often is a requirement for a driver's license, and included in the road test. The steps involved include:

1. Pull parallel to the curb and one car width away from it. Normally, you will pull alongside the car that occupies the space ahead of the space that you want.
2. Check your rearview mirror to make sure the road behind you is clear for backing.
3. Turn your steering wheel clockwise (to the right) and back into the space

slowly until your right-hand mirror is opposite the left rear bumper of the car in the space ahead.

4. Turn your wheel counterclockwise (to the left) and slowly back the remaining distance into the space.

5. You may end up at the back of the space. If so, turn your wheels so they are parallel to the curb and move forward until you are in the center of the space. Your car should be no more than one foot from the curb.

6. Look both ways before you open your car door and exit your car.

7. When exiting the parking space, put on your turn signal or flashers.

These steps require practice in order to know exactly how much to turn the steering wheel. A good way to practice parallel parking is to take your car to a vacant parking lot. Set two rubbish cans 22 feet apart, and six feet from an edge of the lot. The cans will represent the corners of cars occupying the spaces ahead and behind the parking space that you wish to use.

Several car manufacturers now offer automated parallel parking features.

Head-In Parking
As mentioned, head-in parking includes both right-angle parking and diagonal parking. In right-angle parking, your car is parked at a right angle to the traffic flow. In diagonal parking, your car is parked at some other angle, typically 45 degrees.

Right-Angle Parking
Right-angle parking is the most used configuration today. The width of the parking spaces and the width of the aisles determine the ease of parking in right-angle spaces. Supermarkets often have wider spaces to ease the loading of groceries. Parking garages will have tighter dimensions because the spaces are so much more costly to build. For some reason, hospital parking lots often provide narrow spaces despite the fact that visitors often are infirm and have difficulty getting in and out of their vehicles.

The best way to get into a tight space is to back in, especially if the aisle is narrow. You may have a passenger get out of the car and assist you if you do this, as you may not be able to see how close you are to the adjoining cars. If you pull in, you can see more clearly how close you are to the car on the driver's side. But backing out of the space must be done with care. Be sure to use your flashers as you back out.

Other Angle (Diagonal) Parking
Reversing out of a parking space can be dangerous. However, diagonal parking, such as 45-degree parking, is the most dangerous because your line of sight is blocked by adjoin-

ing vehicles until you have backed into and blocked the travel lane. Any angle parking on public streets should be considered dangerous. This is in contrast to exiting a parallel space where you have a clear view of traffic from your left side mirror. As with right-angle parking, activate your flashers as you leave a diagonal space. And take note, it is illegal to back into these spots.

Parking Garages

Legend has it that four older and very experienced traffic engineers were writing a manual on various design aspects of parking. Their research did not turn up a maximum practical number of levels for a garage. In desperation, they drove their sedan to the top of a very high garage with circular ramps. Then, they sped back down the ramps as fast as they could. Round and round they went. As they careened past the sixth floor from the top, the engineer in the back right seat lost his cookies. And that is how the standard for the maximum number of floors in a parking garage was determined. Fortunately, the numbers of levels in a garage are limited today and there are fewer circular exit ramps.

As you enter a garage, note the location of the door, stairway, or elevator that you will use to leave the garage. Do this as soon as you can after you enter the garage. You will want to park as close to this exit as possible, especially if you have luggage or, on the return, shopping bags. Often, you can get closer to the stairway or elevator by going to an upper level of the garage.

Choosing Parking Spaces

If you are in a large parking lot with multiple aisles, it is often possible to pull through one space and occupy the adjoining space in the next aisle over. This way your car is facing out into the aisle and no backing is required. In both large lots and garages, write down your aisle number and keep it in your wallet or purse. Or, buy a locater gizmo that hangs on your key chain. At night, park near lights. And, by all means, avoid parking under bird nests or roofs covered with ice.

Passing

Look for a Clear Lane

Before you pull out to pass, make sure that the passing lane is clear. To do this, check your rearview mirrors. Then, check the blind spot to your left and just behind you. The procedure also should be followed when driving on a multi-lane freeway.

Get a Running Start

It is difficult to pass a car that is going near your speed. To do so, lay back until you are approaching a passing zone. Speed up before reaching the zone so you are going at passing speed as soon as you enter the zone. Be aware that some passing zones were delineated at a time when most vehicles traveled more slowly. If so, there may not be enough room to pass in the marked zone. Pull back in behind the vehicle that you're following as soon as you run out of space. If you are the second of two cars passing another vehicle, do not pull up next to the vehicle you are passing until you are sure that the first passing vehicle is going fast enough to both clear the passed vehicle *and* leave enough space for you to pull in behind it.

Go Past the Overtaken Vehicle as Quickly as Possible

Some drivers go slowly on stretches of road such as curves and hills where passing is not allowed. Then, as they see the clear road associated with a passing zone, they speed up. Be prepared for this and abort your passing move if their unexpected acceleration puts you in jeopardy.

When passing, leave at least three feet of side clearance between your vehicle and any vehicle that you are passing.[43] Once you are past, look in your rearview mirror (not the side-view) and pull in only when you can see both headlights of the vehicle that you have just passed.

Set Wipers on High Beforehand

Say it is raining and you are passing a tractor-trailer. The spray from his rear wheels can blind you if you don't turn your wipers on high before passing. Be sure to pass quickly so you have time to react in case a situation occurs in front of you after you start to pass. Oncoming Vehicle? Abort Immediately.

Aborting a pass means jamming on your brakes and pulling in behind the vehicle you are attempting to pass. Things can get hairy if the person you are passing slows down at the same time, or if another person is right behind you. Be sure to check your rearview mirror before passing. You are probably better off waiting and letting the driver behind you pass first if she appears to be in a hurry.

Give Way, Don't Speed Up

If you are being passed, make the job of the passing driver as easy as possible. Do not speed up. Instead, slow down slightly. If it looks like she won't make it, slow down quickly so she has room to pull in front of you. Don't slow down if the person tries to pull in behind you. If a really dangerous situation develops, you may have to take the shoulder.

If you are approaching a passing vehicle from the other direction, and she is in your lane, hit the brakes hard and take the shoulder. After all, you are closing at a probable speed of over 100 miles per hour and there is little time to wait and see how the situation will play out.

Conversely, heaven forbid, if you are the idiot who is passing in such a way as to collide with an oncoming vehicle, don't swerve to your left and block their escape route. Remember, the road is probably twenty- to twenty-four-feet wide. In a pinch, the vehicles getting out of the way may be able to free up enough width in the center of the highway for you to get through if their vehicles are only partially on the shoulder. However, all bets are off if you're sliding sideways. For a further discussion, see Chapter 8, "Emergencies."

Passing Slow Vehicles
Farm machinery and heavy construction equipment travel very slowly (See the section of this chapter entitled "Farm Machinery"). You must brake as soon as you see them. And, as the driver of a slow vehicle, you should be aware of the traffic behind you. A courteous driver will pull to the side and stop to let an accumulated conga line of cars by. This is a common practice among school bus drivers. Be hesitant to pass if you are in a no passing zone and cannot see oncoming vehicles.

Wet or Icy Conditions
Passing requires a higher speed and two lane changes. In winter, the left hand or passing lane of a four-lane freeway may not be plowed as well as the right-hand or main travel lane. This means that you are much more likely to lose traction and slide sideways when passing in wet or icy conditions.

At Night, Use Low Beams If You Are Being Passed
At night, courtesy calls for you to have your low beams on as you approach a car from the rear. Your low beams do not travel as far as the high beams, but you can use the beams of the vehicle that you are passing to assist your sight. Once you are past the car you should turn on your high beams. You are probably going fast and need more light to see a safe distance ahead. If you are in the car being passed, dim your lights so you do not blind the passing driver.

Observe the Speed Limit at All Times
And now for the kicker, exceeding the speed limit is illegal, *even when passing*. If the car in front of you is going at or close to the speed limit, it is prudent to stay a safe distance behind. How many times have you passed someone only to have that car catch up to you at the next traffic light? Even on the open road, the time savings are not that significant.

Also see the section on conga lines earlier in this chapter and the discussion at the end of Chapter 8, "Emergencies," concerning an oncoming car that swerves into your lane.

Police

First and foremost, police are here for our safety. I often think of the police when I recall how I felt seeing a woman killed in front of my eyes by a person running a red light (see Foreword). Imagine how they must feel when they see the same thing day in and day out, people being killed by the stupidity of others. Know the phone number for your police. It is usually 911. As you enter another state, you may see that state's emergency number posted on the side of the highway. If it is not 911, memorize it while you are driving in that state.

The Case of the Identical License Plates

I treat all police with the utmost respect. And I never underestimate their intelligence. They are keen observers of human nature as well as being versed in the law. Back in my youth, the State of Ohio issued new license plates each year. An annual registration fee was collected and the color of the plate was changed to prevent reuse of old plates. Unknown to us, one of our skinflint neighbors avoided the annual fee by repainting his old plates. This went on until one day when he drove to Cleveland on business. There a passing officer noted that the numbers and letters on his plates matched perfectly with those on the plates of the car parked in front of him.

Assisting the Police

I am especially proud of how my father and his brother helped the law. It was in 1929, my father was 20 and his brother was 18. During the summers, their parents rented a cottage at Point Pleasant on the New Jersey seashore. The family owned a large, open Lincoln touring car with a raised rear seat. However, the local chief of police had no patrol car. Visitors knew this and would hit the gas as they crossed into his jurisdiction. The town fathers had erected a large billboard at this boundary to extol the virtues of a visit to their sleepy community.

It was behind this billboard that my father and his brother waited in "Linky." And, in the elevated back seat sat the chief. As a speeder rushed past, the chief tapped my dad on the shoulder and the chase was on. As this unlikely trio bore down on the errant but unsuspecting motorist, my uncle began madly squeezing the black rubber bulb on the car's large, chrome, three-chime air horn. Many were the surprised speeders as the chief, sitting regally in the high rear seat, pulled alongside and motioned them to the shoulder.

The Speeder Who Invites a Huge Fine

Then there is my cousin, the Porsche owner. He is returning to Boston from Cape Cod on a Sunday evening with his wife in the passenger seat and yours truly stuffed in the back. He begins heading north on Route 3. The process involves shifting gears. It is my first time in the car and I am focused on the shift lever on the floor between the two front seats. He goes from first to second and I am slightly pressed back against the seat. The pressure becomes more like an impact from firing a shotgun when he goes from second to third but the ride is still very smooth. Even so, I just happen to glance up at the speedometer at this point. I am quite surprised to see the needle rapidly pass 80. Seconds later I hear a siren behind us. My cousin pulls over and soon a trooper ambles up to the driver's window. My cousin rolls it down and, in his gruff manner, says, "What's your problem, Officer?" It was an expensive opening line, and the heavy fine reflected the disrespectful and uncooperative nature of his retort.

Nor is this an unusual incident. Last week our local paper related a chase of a high-speed driver. Twice during the pursuit he saluted the chasing police with his middle finger. He was quickly apprehended and his bail was set at $25,000.

If You Are Pulled Over

This brings us to that inevitable time when you will be pulled over. Here's what you do:

- Pull over promptly (that's probably not a surprise). Do it in a safe spot and make sure you are out of the travel lane.
- Give yourself an attitude adjustment. Don't be furious, impatient to make that appointment that you are late for, or sure that the officer is wrong. Instead, relax, stay calm, and prepare to thank him for stopping you and alerting you to what you have done. Remember, he has probably seen someone killed within the last few weeks because they did the same idiotic thing that you just did, and that includes speeding.
- Turn on your dome light if it is night. Then place both hands on the steering wheel. Don't reach for your registration or proof of insurance until the officer instructs you to do so. Let the officer shine his light in the glovebox before you reach in.
- Never talk over an officer, brag about your connections, or attempt a bribe.

The Kind Officer

You may be lucky. The cop may have a kind heart and only give you a warning. That is what happened to my friend's cousin. He actually was exceeding the speed limit when pulled over. As the cop started to tell the driver why he was stopped, his wife butted in, "Officer, I told him I don't know how many times not to do that." The officer took a second or so to think about her comment. Then he said to the driver, "I'm not going to give you a ticket. You have enough problems already."[44]

Traffic Cameras

One interesting development in law enforcement is the use of cameras to detect traffic violations. One application is at intersections where the cameras can note if you run a red light or made a right turn without coming to a full stop. Others are being used to catch speeders on the open highway. Currently these devices are being used in such places as New Haven, Connecticut; Schaumburg, Illinois; and Phoenix, Arizona. Typically, cameras intended to catch speeders will take a picture of your car if you are exceeding the speed limit by more than 11 miles per hour. Your license plate will be read from the photo and a ticket will be mailed to your home.[45] Traffic cameras are more effective than the full-sized fiberglass policemen that are posted at major intersections in Baotou, China.[46]

Also see the section of this chapter entitled "Speeding."

Railroad Crossings

In the introduction, we discussed the impossibility of two objects occupying the same space at the same time. In the case of railroad tracks, the space on the road above the tracks belongs to the train. Your car is just a visitor. Just because you can't see the train doesn't mean that it's not about to occupy that space. This makes railroad crossings one of the most dangerous of all driving locations. Railroad crossings in just 10 states were the scene of over 2,700 crashes in a single year. Texas was at the top of the list with over 550 collisions followed by Illinois with over 330 car/train crashes. Here are a few other facts and some strategies for you to cross safely.[47]

You Can't Hear a Diesel Locomotive Until It's at the Crossing

The noise of an approaching locomotive does not travel ahead of the train. The only safe way to alert motorists is for the engineer to blow the locomotive's horn as it approaches a grade crossing. The signal sequence is a long blast and two short toots followed by another continuous, long blast as the train reaches the crossing. The crossing gates are supposed to come down. Normally, these two things do happen, but they are not guaranteed. In densely populated areas, some communities have actually tried to talk the railroad out of blowing their horn because it disturbs the neighborhood.

In very rural areas, it is too expensive to install crossing gates, or even flashing lights at all crossings. Some of these crossings are so lightly traveled that the train may not even signal. An example would be a grade crossing that provides a farmer with access to his fields. Here you are on your own. A train can be using any active track, even if the road crossing that track does not have a warning device for motorists.

You Can't Win a Race with a Train

Accidents have happened because people have tried to drive around crossing gates even when they see the train coming. It takes a train over a mile to stop. The train can't stop for you. And, the train is most likely coming too fast for you to outrun it. If there are gates, bells, or flashing lights, wait until they stop. While crossing the tracks immediately after the train goes by may appear to be safe, I have seen a car try this without seeing another train approaching in the opposite direction. In other words the gates may be staying down because another train is coming. The train weighs two thousand times what your car weighs. If it hits you, it finishes you!

Stop, Look, and Listen

If a railroad crossing does not have gates, bells, or flashing lights, you should always stop, look carefully in both directions, and listen (turn the radio off) for the train whistle before crossing. Then cross quickly. And never ever stop with any part of your vehicle within 10 feet of the tracks.

Look for Space on the Far Side of the Tracks

Before crossing, also be sure there is space for your car to occupy on the far side of the tracks. A recent school bus disaster involved a traffic light on the far side of the tracks and vehicles waiting for the light to change. These cars and trucks were backed up to the railroad crossing. The school bus stopped, heard no train, pulled onto the tracks, and stopped just behind the last vehicle in line. The problem was that the bus stopped *on the tracks!* When the bus driver heard the train coming, she had no place to go.

If You Stall On the Tracks

Leave your car immediately. If no train is coming, you can try to push the vehicle off the tracks. If you have a standard transmission, you can probably move it off the tracks by running the starter while the transmission is in first gear. If a train is coming, walk quickly away from the tracks in the direction of the approaching train. This way you will not be struck by pieces of the vehicle when it is struck by the train.[48]

If you have time, you might try to wave down the train. If you have a cellular phone, a better solution is to call 911. The emergency people usually have the number for the railroad's dispatching center. Be sure to include your location when you call.

Reckless Driving

Driving is considered reckless when three conditions are met. First, the driver must consciously and intentionally drive in a dangerous manner. Second, the driver knows or should know that his actions place other people at increased risk. And third, the time of day, location, weather, traffic volume, and vehicle and driver condition make the increased risk obvious and serious. If reckless driving causes the death of another person, the driver can be charged and convicted of vehicular homicide.[49]

Road Rage

Road rage is so surreal as to be unbelievable, yet it occurs. A survey of 2,500 irritated drivers reported that the largest number react to bad driving by honking their horns (43 percent). But 36 percent resort to cursing, 13 percent wave their fist or arms, and 10 percent make an obscene gesture. Seven percent were so angry that they called the police and one percent actually admitted that they had crashed into the car in front of them on purpose. Four percent of the Washington, D.C., respondents to the survey reported that they slammed into another driver's car.[50]

As the survey shows, the road rager is actually willing to put his own life in danger and instigate actions that will seriously damage his car. Here are some suggestions in case you encounter one of them:[51]

- Stay calm and relaxed.
- Make every effort to get out of the way safely. *Do not escalate the situation.*
- Never challenge an aggressive driver by speeding up or attempting to hold your position in your travel lane.
- Avoid eye contact.
- Ignore harassing gestures and refrain from returning them.
- If you are being followed, drive to the nearest police station.

In order to stop this utter nonsense, it is up to each of us to report aggressive drivers to the police immediately. If possible, include a vehicle description, location, license plate number, and direction of travel. If a road rager is involved in a crash, stop a safe distance from the crash scene. When police arrive, describe to them the driving behavior that you observed. Hopefully, some road ragers will realize that understanding, respect, and courtesy, rather than rage, will make their trip safer.

Roundabouts

Roundabouts operate in a counterclockwise direction (clockwise in countries where cars drive on the left). Earlier versions of roundabouts were called rotaries or traffic circles. However, roundabouts are often smaller in diameter, and are specifically designed to "calm" traffic. They do so by causing traffic to slow down. The slower speeds mean that crashes on roundabouts are less likely. When crashes do occur, they are often less severe then at a signalized intersection. Cars also experience fewer delays at roundabouts than at a signalized intersection. This means less fuel consumption and air pollution. Roundabouts are, of course, less expensive to build and maintain than a full interchange with overpasses.[52]

How to Use a Roundabout

Unlike intersections that are regulated by traffic lights, roundabouts require self-regulation. It is the driver already in the circle that has the right-of-way. The arriving driver has to decide when to enter and what lane to select. Upon arriving at a roundabout, the driver must slow or even stop. Next, the driver looks to the left for a gap in oncoming traffic. When a gap appears, the driver enters the roundabout and drives in a left-hand (counterclockwise) direction toward the exit that she wants. As she does, she also watches for traffic entering the roundabout from her right. She then activates her right turn signal just past the exit before the one that she plans to use. These maneuvers require a highly proactive driver, one with eyes in the back of her head! And they can result in a fender bender if the driver is unfamiliar with their operation.

Before You Enter a Roundabout

The most important step in using a roundabout occurs as you approach. It is here that you read the sign that identifies the various exits from the roundabout. Select your exit at this point. This frees you to concentrate on turning and watching for other cars while you are in the roundabout. If you miss your exit, simply go around again until you come to it. Good luck!

Pedestrians

Unlike signalized intersections, pedestrians don't have a "walk only" phase at roundabouts. It is easy to see pedestrians crossing in front of you as you approach the roundabout. However, those crossing your exit lane may be blocked from your view by vehicles in front of you. Moreover, stopping for a pedestrian as you exit the roundabout invites a rear-end collision. The only answer for this is to exercise extreme caution as you leave the roundabout.

Tractor-Trailers

Roundabouts have a small circumference to slow traffic and conserve space. This requires the left rear wheels of tractor-trailers to mount the median curb. The curb is designed to accept the rear double wheels. However, the median is sloped downward from the center for drainage. This tilts the trailer outward. Meanwhile, the tractor cab is on level pavement. What feels like a comfortable speed to the truck driver may be fast enough to flip the trailer.

Signalized Traffic Circles

Several of the older traffic circles in the Boston area have traffic lights controlling the entry to each approach route. These were installed because the volume of arriving vehicles exceeded the capacity of the rotary. It took the guesswork out of when to enter and eliminated conflicts with other entering vehicles once in the circle. This made these older traffic circles safer.

Rumble Strips

Rumble strips are not installed by dentists to check for loose fillings. Instead, they are designed to alert drivers who wander out of their lanes. One popular design resembles tank tread tracks cut into the pavement. These can either be just to the right of the right lane, or in the median. In southern locations, raised reflectors also may be used to delineate the centerline. Rumble strips also are installed across the road to alert drivers that they are approaching tollbooths, an intersection, or a construction area.

School Buses

One day, I came home from school and my mom wasn't there. I was a senior in high school and drove in a car pool. It was a day of horror, for I learned that my mom was in the hospital. When I went in to see her, her entire face was black and blue, one of her eyes was swollen shut, and she was obviously in great pain. It was in the days before seatbelts and she had been in a hurry. She ran the hood of her car under the back of a stopped school bus. The front of the car stopped when it hit the rear axle of the bus. Otherwise she would have been decapitated. As it was, her head went through the windshield. Fortunately no children were hurt. But it gave me a healthy respect for school buses.

Be Prepared to Stop
School buses represent a special driving situation. As they cover their route, they will make stops at random intervals. In the morning, the waiting students give these stops away, but in the afternoon, there may be no one waiting for them. If you see a bus, be prepared to stop. If you don't stop, you may seriously injure or even kill a child. That is why it is the law in all states that cars traveling in both directions must stop. The only possible exception is if you are traveling in the opposite direction on a four-lane divided highway with a median separation (check your state law).

Don't Tailgate
You will rear-end the school bus if it stops suddenly.

School Bus Patterns
Typically the buses pick up students by around 8:30 a.m. and can drop off the kids beginning as early as 2:30 p.m. In the example above, it was a foggy, weekday morning and my mother was not looking for a school bus. As a result, she rear-ended the bus (with no injury to the kids), totaled her car, and spent three days in the hospital.

Kids Are Unpredictable
The bus may have to stop suddenly if there is a disturbance on board and, when getting on or off the bus, kids may dawdle or sprint unexpectedly.

Don't Become Frustrated
In the past, drivers would get very frustrated as the line of motorists behind the bus grew longer and longer. Today, most school districts train their drivers to pull to the side of the road and let motorists pass if a long line forms.

Schools

Speeding in front of a school is dangerous because students, in their exuberance, frequently forget to look out for traffic. For this reason, speed limits are lower and there are often police officers on hand. Note that unless otherwise posted, the speed zone around schools is applicable at any time, day or night.

Sometimes traffic patterns are altered at schools when buses depart. Parents picking up children should be aware of these changes and should have a backup plan if, for some reason, they cannot arrive on time to pick up their children. This is a useful purpose for cell phones and text messaging.

Sleepiness

Falling asleep at the wheel violates our three-second rule for distractions. After three seconds, a person who has fallen asleep is likely to wander into either the ditch or the oncoming lane. Drivers do have some interesting tricks for keeping awake. They slap their face, roll down the window, take off their shoes, or turn up the radio. Unfortunately the American Automobile Association Foundation for Traffic Safety says that these don't work. Instead, pull over and take a nap for a half-hour. When you wake up, walk around and shake off the grogginess. Then get a cup of coffee and go on your way.[53]

Slow Drivers

Are you a slow driver? If so pull off the road into a legal parking space and let others pass when a line forms behind you. Otherwise, you risk being rear-ended. You also should avoid high-speed highways. Instead, travel on slower, alternate routes. Finally, you should consider traveling during those times of day when traffic is light. Just as with speeders, the difference in speed between a slow driver and the other traffic creates a dangerous situation.

Speed Bumps

Speed bumps are built across the road to slow traffic. Speeding over these can put your car out of control so take them *very* slowly. They often are used in areas where children are playing and are a safety measure that is intended to calm traffic. In Jamaica they are called "sleeping policemen."[54]

More recently, speed plateaus (speed humps) have appeared. These are the same height as the speed bumps, but the ones that I have seen are twenty to forty feet long. In my opinion, these are less dangerous if accidentally taken at high speed.

The newest additions to this arsenal of road growths are speed "lumps." These are speed bumps with holes in them that permit the unimpeded passage of emergency vehicles.[55]

Speed Limits

In the USA, we have only recently been able to drive legally at speeds of up to 85 miles per hour. The first speed limit was established in England in 1861. It was ten miles per hour for "light locomotives," the term for early autos in that country. In 1865 it was revised downward to two miles per hour in the city and four miles per hour in the country. That law was most famous, however, for requiring someone to proceed 60 feet in front of the vehicle with a red flag or lantern and, like Paul Revere, warn of the oncoming invader.[56]

A Dangerous Rural Road

A while back, we talked about dangerous roads. Obviously, we want to drive in a way that keeps our car safely on the highway. However, the correct speed for safe travel is not always obvious.

There was an example of a dangerous country road in front of our farmhouse in Ohio, a road that looked perfectly safe for speeding. As you approached the house from the north, the road climbed quickly and began a gradual curve to the right. It then became level and straight as it passed our place. At the posted speed the road was perfectly safe. But if a car came racing over the lip of the hill, it would become momentarily airborne. In that instant, it lost all traction. Normally, tires would squeal, brakes would be hit, and the driver would regain control of the vehicle. However, summer rainstorms made the road slick. Then, the car stayed in the air long enough to turn slightly sideways. Any application of brakes would put the rear of the auto into a skid to the left as it landed. The first impulse of the driver was to crank the steering wheel hard to the left. The rear end would then fishtail over to the right and the car would begin a sideways skid down the right shoulder of the road.

The speeder instinctively would swing the wheel back to the right. Then one of two things would happen. Sometimes the tires caught and the car returned to the pavement and sped off. If not, the vehicle continued its skid into our mailbox and the tall, thick hedge beyond it. It would come to a stop and my dad would appear and promise not to report the crash if the driver would supply him with a new mailbox.

Of course, a very, very fast driver would not be quite so fortunate. His car would shoot across the road, go over the embankment on the left and land in a hay field. The road is still there 50 years later, and the fastest of the speeders still end up in that field when it rains! And our old home still seems to acquire a new mailbox once or twice a year.

Unsafe at High Speeds

Even perfectly straight and level roads are dangerous for speeders. The family of a high school girlfriend drove me to a picnic one sunny afternoon. On our return trip, we took the Ohio Turnpike. The girl's mother was driving and the car was brand new. Being somewhat of a free spirit, she decided to see how fast the car could go. As we hit 90 miles per hour the car became partially airborne and began to float lazily from side to side. My friend and I were in the back seat and were scared to death. The girl's father finally got his wife to slow down before she lost control and the car rolled over. It is *not* something to do.

Speed can produce some other interesting effects as well. Back in the era of bench seats, teenage drivers would speed around curves to the right in order to get their date to slide up against them. Then there was my cousin who liked to bounce up and down on the back seat of my mother's 1946 Ford convertible. One day she descended into a steep dip at high speed. My cousin was descending from a huge bounce just as the car's springs bottomed out. The impact sent him flying up and his head went right through the canvas roof. These anecdotes have happy endings. But make no mistake, "speed kills."

How Speed Limits Are Determined

One way is for traffic engineers to measure the speeds of vehicles at a point along the road. They then set a speed that is only exceeded by 15 percent of the vehicles. Speed limits determined using this practical approach account for driver adjustments for the design of that highway. As such, they will result in less speeding than speed limits that are set arbitrarily.

In some instances, speed limits become a political football. If the speed limit is arbitrarily set extremely low for a location, the location may become more dangerous. Why? Because some motorists will adhere to the low limit while others will travel at a higher but safe speed. There will now be significant differences in speed and that may actually cause more accidents.

The same speed limits also may be found for widely varying conditions. For example, the speed limits on parts of US 301 north of Ocala, Florida, and on Route 316 between Atlanta and Athens, Georgia, are both 65 miles per hour. However, the conditions are quite different. The parts of US 301 that are signed for 65 miles per hour are completely rural with infrequent, narrow country roads with stop signs. However, Route 316 is characterized by busy, closely spaced intersections with traffic lights.

In the past, some states have legislated slower speeds for trucks on freeways because they were unsafe if operated at the same speed as cars. Again, the difference in speeds between the two types of vehicles may actually decrease the overall safety of that expressway, particularly if the terrain is reasonably level and the overtaking driver is not familiar with the dual speed limits. Fortunately modern trucks can, for the most part (exception: steep uphills), keep up with autos and such legislation is less necessary.

Maximum Speed Limits

The maximum speed limit in the United States is 85 miles per hour.[57] This is permitted in parts of southwest Texas. There are now three states with maximum speed limits of 80 miles per hour. Eleven states have maximum speed limits of 75 miles per hour, and twenty-two states have speed limits of 70 miles per hour. Most of the remaining states have maximum speed limits of 65 miles per hour.[58] Those drivers from states with speed limits of 65 miles per hour or less are quite likely to find it uncomfortable to travel at the higher speed limits.

Ranges of Speed Limits

There is a wide variability in speed limits so it is always wise to check the signs as you toot along. Here are the current ranges:[59]

Residential Streets	15–30 mph
Urban arterial roads	35–45
Major highways in cities	50–65
Rural 2-lane roads	45–65
Rural expressways	55–70
Rural interstates	65–85

Table 5: Ranges of speed limits

Nighttime Speed Limits

Some locations in Florida have lower speed limits at night. For example, a rural road posted for 60 miles per hour in daylight might show a nighttime speed limit of 45 miles per hour. This is especially helpful for senior drivers. It is also designed to save the lives of wandering alligators.

Don't Speed

As most of us know, the white signs represent legal speed limits. Exceeding these limits exposes the driver to an expensive traffic ticket and points on their license. While this sounds trite, once a driver gets two speeding tickets, he is usually in danger of losing his license and that is not trite.

In countries like Switzerland the cost of the traffic ticket is based on both speed and income of the driver. In 2010 the driver of a Mercedes Benz SLS AMG was fined over a million dollars for doing 180 miles per hour on a road between Bern and Lausanne.[60]

On freeways, one often senses that the police will not normally ticket someone who is only 5 miles or so above the speed limit. However, speeds even slightly above the speed limits in downtown areas or in front of schools often yield fines if the radar is on. Nor should one expect to see the radar gun in time to slow. After many years of experience, the police have selected ideal spots to see you before you notice them. Beware especially of cresting or descending a hill at excessive speed.

Conversely, uphills seem to be relative free of speed traps. However, the police, like a guilty conscience, can appear in many unexpected places. I've been pulled over by a policeman driving an ambulance. And I've seen an officer standing in a bus stop shelter with a handheld radar gun. The first person in this country to be pulled over was Jacob German, a New York City cab driver. In 1899, he was driving his electric car down Lexington Avenue at a blistering 12 miles per hour in an 8-mile-per-hour zone. A police officer on a bicycle promptly arrested him and threw him in jail.[61]

Kinetic Energy and Traffic Deaths

Be aware that the higher the speed, the less likely that you will survive an accident. The kinetic energy generated by your car is directly proportional to the *square* of your speed. Deaths in traffic accidents go up with speed at an even faster rate. And, finally, a speeder in a traffic flow creates large differences in relative speeds with other autos, which is highly dangerous.

Speeding Up While Passing

Details on how to pass another car are in the section of this chapter entitled "Passing." If the car that you are passing is moving at the speed limit, you will be breaking the law. If you still want to pass a slower driver you may have to temporarily become a speeder to get safely around him. As mentioned elsewhere in the text, the difference between your speed and the speed of the other vehicles creates an unsafe situation.

Cars and Roads Not Designed to Exceed Posted Speed

Speed limits are based on the design of the road and the car. On curves, the limits are set well below the speed at which tires will lose side-to-side traction on dry pavement. That is why yellow advisory signs that indicate reduced speeds appear in advance of sharp curves. A driver who attempts to round the curve at a higher speed can easily lose control of his car. In the past, car suspension systems could not tolerate speeds in the seventies and would tend to float or careen from side to the side at higher speeds. While many of the larger modern cars can provide a more acceptable ride at these speeds, they are still extremely susceptible to rollover accidents if over-steered.

Few motorists realize that a very dangerous place to speed is around the outside of curves on rural roads. These roads have a high crown, which means the pavement of the outside lane slopes severely down from the centerline to the outside of the curve. This makes your car more susceptible to a roll over. Instead, slow down before entering the curve.

Pass Parked Emergency Vehicles Safely

It makes good sense to slow down or move over when passing a parked emergency vehicle such as a police car, ambulance, or fire truck. After several fatal accidents, Florida enacted a law requiring approaching cars to vacate the lane closest to the emergency vehicle when there are two or more lanes in the same direction. Otherwise the law requires that you slow to 20 miles per hour below the posted speed limit. If the speed limit is 25 miles per hour or less, you must slow to 5 miles per hour on a two-lane road. Most other states have adopted similar legislation.

As Road Conditions Deteriorate, Safe Speeds Are Well Below the Posted Limit

In other words, a highway posted for 55 miles per hour may not be safe to travel at speeds above 25 miles per hour in slick or icy conditions. You should be aware that you are subject to a speeding ticket if an officer determines that you are traveling at an unsafe speed *even if it is below the posted speed limit*. These types of tickets are issued automatically if you cause an accident.

Don't "Underceed" the Speed Limits Either

Driving well below the speed limit poses a hazard for other drivers. That is why you will see a minimum speed limit of 40 miles per hour posted on express highways. In western states and some parts of Europe, the high speed limits mean that you must increase the distance ahead that you are "Scouting" from the 513 feet or over 30 car lengths suggested in Chapter 1 to about 600 feet (35 car lengths or two football fields). Particularly dangerous are slow-moving trucks or farm vehicles (prohibited on interstates) because you come up to them so much more quickly than other vehicles traveling at a similar rate to yours. That's why signs on I-81 in Virginia read "Trucks and Combination Vehicles Use Right Lane When Operated Below 65 Miles Per Hour."

If you have to drive more slowly than the speed limit, you should use the climbing lane where it is provided. Turn on your flashers and watch your rearview mirror. If an unaware driver comes upon you too quickly, you may have to take the shoulder to avoid a rear-end collision.

Do you notice that the danger of differences in speed is a recurrent theme throughout this book? Also see the sections of this chapter entitled "Conga Lines," "Slow Drivers," and "Speed Traps."

Speed Traps

Speed traps are places where motorists are not informed in advance that speed limits are very strictly enforced. As of this writing, allegedly one of the most notorious speed traps is located on US Route 301 north of Starke, Florida. Route 301 runs diagonally from the Jacksonville area towards Tampa and is a favored route by motorists who come down the East Coast and are headed for Florida's Gulf resorts. This particular speed trap is one of many noted on a website on this subject.

Large billboards (erected by others) several miles before the town announce the speed trap. This is soon followed by a smaller, more apologetic sign that says something like "We are doing it for safety." On my last trip through the town I spotted three separate white patrol cars hidden behind various signs and buildings. There was another cruiser lurking at a town slightly further south on Route 301. In both communities, the traffic was moving exactly at the speed limit.

Clues for the Clueless

More often, you will receive a clue that the police are especially diligent in enforcing the speed limit in a specific area. For example, there may be signs such as "Radar In Use," "Speed Limit Enforced By Aircraft," or "Speed Limits Strictly Enforced." Or there may be a portable radar unit with a huge digital display of your speed. However, my favorites are the signs on state highways in Georgia that read "Speed Checked by Detection Devices." Eyeballing speeds never did work!

No Clues?

What would I advise if you don't recall seeing a speed limit sign as you come into a village? Well, it is always best to slow down, particularly if your car has an out-of-state license plate. Your other option would be to go at the speed of the rest of the traffic, providing that it is no more than five miles per hour above the posted limit. But you don't want to attempt that in that Florida town on Route 301.

Stop Signs

One of life's experiences to be avoided at all costs is a drive through downtown Boston. Even in perfect daylight and with dry pavement you start off with two strikes against you. The first is the narrow, twisting streets of that fair city and the second is the outrageous behavior of Boston's drivers.

I especially recall another of my poor mother's experiences. She was driving me through downtown Boston with the intent of showing me her favorite college haunts. We were on a one-way street when we came to an intersection with another one-way street with traffic flowing from right to left. That street had a stop sign. We slowed and proceeded through the intersection. As we did, we noticed that the sidewalks were quite narrow and some utility equipment was parked along the other street in such a position that we couldn't see if traffic was approaching from that direction.

We weren't worried because we could see that their street did have a stop sign. What we didn't realize was that motorists on that street couldn't see our car because of that same utility equipment. *Wham!* A car zoomed out of the side street and slammed into the right front fender of our car. The crash brought the patrons out of the bar at the corner. They were disappointed to see that there were no injuries. Just as they were walking back in, a burly bartender in a dirty white apron emerged, wiped his hands on the apron, and said to us, "That's the third time this week." Fortunately, we could still drive the car. So here are a few tips for stop signs:

Come to a **Complete** *Stop*

Of all the advice in this book, coming to a complete stop at a stop sign is probably the most important. Do you really come to a complete stop? Or, do you roll through slowly, thinking that you can stop in time if you need to? If the latter, please try an experiment at your next stop sign. As you roll through, pretend that you do see an oncoming car and slam on your brakes. Where did the front of your car stop? In the intersection? You are dead meat. A friend of mine has been completely paralyzed and unable to speak for 18 years because he rolled one too many stop signs. You see, the driver on the main drag does not expect you to pull out and can't avoid you. In fact they actually may prefer to hit you on the passenger side of their car (but the driver side of your car) at 50 miles per hour rather than swerving to the left, and risking being hit head-on by someone else at a combined speed of 100 miles per hour. Think about it.

Look Twice

My neighbor got hit because the sun was in his eyes when he looked to his left and he did not see the van speeding toward him. The reason for looking twice is that you may note movement. This will help you to see something coming through glare. Or see a white car on a snowy day. Or see a motorcycle when all you expected to see was a car. If you look twice, you'll either pick up the motion or your memory will tell you that something has moved since your first glance.

Look in Both Directions

Once, while on foot, I barely escaped serious injury when I looked only in the direction from which traffic was expected. It happened like this. I came to a New York City crosswalk on a one-way street, stopped, and looked in the direction of oncoming traffic. Seeing no cars, I started to cross. As I took my first step, out of the corner of my eye, I suddenly spotted motion from the other direction and, with the reflexes of a 24-year-old, leapt backwards just as a grocery boy with a heavy bike and a huge basket of groceries zoomed through the space that I had just occupied. An older person wouldn't have had a chance.

Don't Trust the Other Driver's Turn Signals

A classical stop sign accident is noting that the approaching driver's right-hand blinker is on and assuming she is going to turn right. I once sat on a civil jury in a state where you had the law on your side if you assumed that the blinker assured you that the approaching vehicle would turn. That is absurd. All it means is that the blinker is blinking. Please wait until that vehicle actually begins to turn before you enter the intersection!

Wait **Behind** *the Stop Line*

As mentioned elsewhere, be sure to wait behind the stop line before entering an intersection. The line is painted in a location that allows cars entering from your right and turning left to pass safely in front of you. As a courtesy, you might even stop a short distance behind the stop line. This helps the people turning in front of you as they are often turning through gaps in oncoming traffic.

Entering the Intersection

When you enter an intersection, you can go straight across or turn left or right. If you are going straight across, do so promptly. This is because you are at risk of being broadsided by a car approaching from a side street that ignores the traffic light or stop sign.

If you are turning left, you should enter the left side of the lane but not occupy the lane in the opposite direction. If you are turning right, do so without swinging wide and entering the lane of oncoming traffic. Otherwise, you are unexpectedly occupying road space that you should not be in. This maneuver, termed "bellying out," is unnecessary for missing the curb and is very unsafe. See the section in Chapter 5 entitled "Right-of-Way" and the sections "Roundabouts" and "Turns" in this chapter.

Traffic from Side Streets

As you are driving down the main road, always watch for cars approaching from side streets. Never feel safe about driving through an intersection until you actually see an approaching vehicle stopped at the stop sign. Perhaps you've heard the expression that two ships are on a "collision course." This is true at an intersection if as you watch an approaching car on the side street it stays at the same point in your vision, like, say, just ahead of the right windshield corner post. As the approaching car slows down for the stop sign, its position will change (it will fall off to the right side of your field of vision) and the risk of a crash is reduced.

Nevertheless, always be ready if a car does pull out of a stop sign into your lane. As you approach the intersection, note if there is room for you to take the shoulder and go behind it. Driving manuals say that this is usually much safer than swerving to the left, entering the opposing lane, and risking a head on crash.

"No-Stop Tom"

There was no right shoulder, only a curb, in Troy, New York, one winter afternoon when I was driving a friend's car eastbound on Route 7. Actually, it was his dad's car and it was brand new. Suddenly, I noticed a car running a stop sign on an intersecting street that angled in on my right. As I slammed on the brakes, his left front fender severely dented the right front fender of my friend's Chevy. I jumped out, examined the damage, and concluded that our car was still operable. An elderly man hobbled out of the other car, looked at our crumpled fender, apologized profusely and said, "If you follow me, I'll take you to my insurance agent."

"How far is that?"

"Two blocks."

"OK."

He turned down a side street and stopped at the third house on the right. He got out of his car and I got out of the Chevy. We walked up to the front door and rang the doorbell. A well-attired, middle-aged gentleman opened the door, saw the elderly man, cast a glance toward the Chevy's dented fender and muttered disgustedly, "Oh no, Tom, not again." And that is when I learned that you must not assume that other drivers will behave predictably. I remember it especially well because I felt responsible for the new car's smashed fender.

Also see the section in Chapter 5 entitled "Right-of-Way," and the section in this chapter entitled "Intersections."

Sun in Your Eyes

It is incredibly dangerous to suddenly come over a hill and be blinded by sunlight. Termed "solar glare," this often happens just after sunrise and shortly before sunset. Its blinding effect is often intensified by a layer of film that builds up on the inside of your windshield. The first thing to do is slow down. Flip down your window visor if you haven't already done so. Even quicker, use your flattened hand to block the sun. Also, try to look down and to the right side of the road and use the white line to guide you. That is the same white line that you use at night when oncoming headlights blind you. Throughout this process be acutely aware of the gap between you and the vehicle in front of you. They also may be blinded and are likely to hit their brakes.

Other sources of glare can include oncoming headlights, paper on the dashboard, a snow-covered landscape, flashing advertisement signs, rain that amplifies glare, flood lights on a business next to the road, and failure to dim your own headlights in fog.[62]

If you are driving away from the sun and are turning at an intersection be aware that the sun may be blinding oncoming drivers and they may not see you attempting to turn.

Tolls

There are a wide variety of bridges, tunnels, turnpikes, and parkways that charge tolls, all the way from the Maine Turnpike to the Golden Gate Bridge.

Toll Collection

Today, tolls are collected in three ways. The old standby, the toll collector, is there if you do not have the exact change. If you do have the right change, you may be able to use any exact change lanes that are available. More recently, toll authorities have gone to automated systems such as "E-ZPass" in the Northeast and Midwest. These systems read a tag on your car electronically and allow you to pass through the booths without stopping, providing your account is paid up. (If not, your picture is taken and your traffic ticket arrives in the mail.)

Barrier Tollbooths

The barrier tollbooths that extend across a superhighway can be dangerous because motorists do not realize how fast they are traveling as they approach the booths. For this reason, it is a good idea to watch for rear-enders by glancing in your rearview mirror several times as you slow for tollbooths.

Hazardous Driver Actions on Toll Plazas

It is very dangerous to weave across a toll plaza just because your car is not lined up for the tollbooth of your choice. You can control this by paying close attention to the signs as you approach. However, you may encounter others who weave frantically in front of you. Either they missed the signs or they are intent on beating as many cars as possible to the booths. Another hazard is the motorist who signifies their objection to tolls by flinging their coins at the exact change basket and missing. If you are doing exact change, slow down, reach your hand over the basket, and carefully drop in your coins. A final danger is motorists who speed through the automated lanes. Toll personnel cross these lanes on foot when they change shifts.

Leaving the Tollbooth

As you leave the tollbooth, be aware of cars weaving in front of you to get to their desired exit ramp. If you are familiar with the tollbooths, you can usually preselect the lane that works best for you. You may actually do this on the basis of the lane that you want after you go through the tolls. Your safest path through tollbooths probably is the extreme right lane if you can pay your toll at the booth in that lane.

Tornadoes

Unlikely as it may seem, some people actually take their car for a drive during a tornado warning (unlike a tornado watch, a tornado warning means one is probably headed your way). If you are that foolish and a tornado is coming toward your car, you are in very grave danger. There are many different suggestions offered for your safety but none are guaranteed. One is that you stop your car so it is facing the oncoming tornado, buckle your seat belt, leave the engine on, keep your head down below the windows, and cover your head with your hands and a blanket.[63]

Traffic Lights

As we wait for a red light to change, we often wonder how long this unwanted delay will last. The short answer? Probably less than a minute. Before being more specific, it is necessary to explain that traffic lights are designed to safely move cars through busy intersections. The simplest intersections are of two one-way streets. Here you have signals controlling both streets. As we all know (I hope) the signal indications are green, yellow, and red. When one street has a green signal, the other street shows red. In fact it stays red not only while the first street goes to yellow, but one second into the red as well. This is a safety feature and works quite well in most areas of our country (also see the section of this chapter entitled "Intersections").

Meaning and Mounting

Traffic signals control traffic flow and indicate which driver has the right-of-way. A red light tells you not to enter the intersection. A yellow light means that your permission to enter the intersection is expiring and a green light means that you may enter the intersection.

On vertical signals, the red light is on the top, the yellow light is in the middle and the green light is at the bottom. When signals are mounted horizontally, the red light is at the left, the yellow light is in the middle and the green light is at the right. These standard arrangements assist the colorblind.

A flashing red light means that you must stop and proceed only when it is safe to do so. A flashing yellow light tells you to slow down and proceed with caution.

The Signal Cycle

The cycle time for a signal is the total time from when your light changes from red to green until it again changes from red to green. Cycle times usually are 90 seconds. If both roads are given equal green time then both phases of the cycle would be the same, and the green time for us in a 90-second cycle would be 41 seconds with three more for yellow and one for safety. Thus, if we arrive just as our light turns yellow, we have to wait 49 seconds until it turns green again.

Now let's say that the streets are two-way and left turns are allowed. At these intersections, traffic engineers throw in a phase for left hand turns on each street. This causes our wait time to go up and our green time to go down. When total cycle times are held to a maximum of 90 seconds, the time for each individual movement becomes less. Modern signal equipment can lengthen the cycle time when traffic flows increase.

Approaching a Green Light

Why is it helpful to be aware of the cycle length? Well, let's say you are several hundred yards from an intersection and you see the light turn green. Will you be able to get through before it turns yellow? You can start counting down the seconds. The higher your count the more you should slow and be prepared to stop. You are approaching what is referred to as an "old" light. And, most lights are programmed for a much smaller amount of green time than 41 seconds.

Approaching a Red Light

If, on the other hand, you are approaching a red light, you can count it down. Why not approach the light slowly rather than racing up to it and grinding to a halt? You may be able to reach the intersection just as it turns green and continue without coming to a stop. This saves fuel and reduces air pollution.

Some of the newer traffic signals have an electronic sensor to control the signal for the lesser-used streets of the intersection. When approaching this type of signal, pull to within four to five feet of the stop line. This is where the detection loop that activates the signal is buried in the pavement. This type of signal is often found in suburban and rural areas.

Waiting for a Green Light

How about when you are already stopped and waiting for a light to turn green? How do you know when it will? If you look closely, you may be able to see the light for the other traffic. If yours is the next phase, you *may* get the go ahead four seconds after the yellow for the other traffic comes on, depending on how the various phases of that particular signal are programmed. *But make absolutely sure that the light actually changes to green before you enter the intersection!*

Say you are way back in a line waiting for the light to turn green. You are concerned as to whether you will get through the intersection before the light turns red again. To help you decide, start counting off the seconds after the light does turn green. If you are up to 15 to 20 seconds and still not at the intersection you should probably be prepared to stop and wait for the next cycle.

You can also estimate how long before you will arrive at the intersection after the light turns green. Count the number of cars ahead of you and multiply by two or three. This will give you the number of seconds that it will take for you to reach the intersection.

Traffic Slugs

Another aspect of traffic lights is the slugs of closely bunched cars that they generate. A street downstream of the light may be clear of traffic and all of the sudden the light will turn green and a stream of cars will appear. If you come to the street from a side street, and you see a slug of cars blocking your entry to the road, just relax and wait until it passes. One interesting place where traffic light slugs can occur is on freeway entrance ramps. If you are zooming down the freeway and see the slug descending a ramp into your lane, you should consider moving to the left lane. These slugs can actually clog a freeway in rush hours (see the section of this chapter entitled "Freeway Driving and Interchanges").

Red-Light Runners and the Three-Second Delay

There have been recent epidemics of red-light running in two or three areas of the country. Crashes with red-light runners are extremely dangerous. Typically, the oncoming car strikes your vehicle on the side, a location where the car body cannot easily absorb the forces generated in the collision. Cars with side air bags fare better, but the impact forces are so strong that you are still likely to be either killed or severely injured. Often the offending driver speeds up to run the light, resulting in a crash at over 50 miles per hour. Keep an eye out for red-light runners in your area. They may be more frequent during holiday seasons. If you notice them often, or if a car in the adjacent lane blocks your view, your best defense may be to wait three to four seconds after the light turns green before entering an intersection.

Trucks

Drivers need to take special precautions when driving near large trucks. Truckers are very experienced drivers. However, the size and weight of their rigs present challenges to other motorists. Trucks have bigger blind spots and need more room to maneuver. It takes longer to pass them and guess who is going to be the loser in a collision. Each year, over 250,000 crashes involve at least one car and one large truck. In more than 70 percent of all truck-car crashes, the person operating the auto is at fault. And in four out of five crashes that result in fatalities, the car driver is killed.[64]

Tailgating Truck
Always let a tailgating truck pass you.

Wet Pavement
To insure your longevity when there is wet pavement (rain, slush, or snow), turn your wipers on high before passing or being passed by a big truck. Tractor-trailers are not the only vehicles that will throw a lot of water or slush onto your windshield. Others with high clearances include delivery trucks and large pickups as well as some SUVs (see the sections of this chapter entitled "Passing" and "Windshield Wipers").

Bow Wave
You also should grip your steering wheel tightly with two hands when you pass the front of a large truck (or as it passes you). The reason? Large trucks create a bow wave of air that spews out to the sides, air that will try to push your car to the opposite side of your lane from the truck. The bow wave will especially affect any box-shaped trailer that you are towing (see the section of this chapter entitled "Wind").

Blind Spots
The sign that you see on the back of trucks, "If you can't see my mirrors, I can't see you," is true. In fact the big rigs have larger blind spots on both sides and the rear. Pass quickly. It is unsafe to stay in these blind spots on either side for a long time. The trucker may need

to change lanes in a hurry for reasons of which you are totally unaware.[65] That is one of the reasons that you are strongly discouraged from passing a truck on the right, particularly when it is swinging out to the left. It may be doing so to make a right-hand turn.

Passing a Conga Lines of Trucks

Someday when you are driving on a freeway, you will come upon a line of closely spaced trucks in the right-hand lane. These drivers are drafting each other just like bicycle riders in the Tour de France. But unlike bicyclists, the truckers in the back are also using their draft to push the truck in front of them. It can be very exciting if you decide to pass them. When one pulls out, it loses its draft and slows down.[66] It will then take forever for that truck to forge to the head of the line and pull back into the right lane. In the meantime, the cars behind it will be delayed. That's why you might plan to pass the trucks on an uphill of the freeway before one pulls out into your lane.

Loose Loads

While small trucks are more likely offenders, be on the lookout for loose loads on any vehicle in front of you. My favorite is the king-sized mattress tied with twine to the roof of a compact sedan.

Exit Ramps

When exiting a freeway, give that tractor-trailer or bus ahead of you plenty of space. It is easy for them to flip over if they exit at too high a speed.

Tunnels

The width of the lanes in tunnels often is narrower than the width of the approaching highways, requiring special concentration on the part of the driver. This can be especially dangerous if the driver's eyes do not adjust quickly to the lack of sunlight in the tunnel. That's why it's good to remove your sunglasses and slow down as you enter.

Turns

The safest way to leave a driveway or parking lot is to come to a stop at the main road with your car at a 90-degree angle to the highway. This enables you to easily see oncoming traffic in both directions. Be sure to look twice in both directions (see the section of this chapter entitled "Stop Signs").

Using Your Turn Signals

If you are turning off a main highway, you must first signal your intentions. The law as to when to begin signaling varies from state to state. As a general rule of thumb, on the open highway you should hit your blinkers at least 500 feet before the turn. If already in the proper lane, begin your signal at least 100 feet from the turn. After you turn, check to see that your turn signals are off.

"Bellying Out"

One error that many drivers make is to "belly out" when turning off the main road into a side street or driveway. That is, they move to the left first before turning right. They do this because they fear hitting the right curb. Bellying out is very dangerous, as it puts them in the adjoining travel lane, a place where other drivers do not expect them to be. The initial move to the left also might suggest to a following driver that the first driver actually is turning left. The following driver may then attempt to pass on the right, hitting the first driver in the right front of their car just as they begin their turn to the right!

Drivers whose rigs overhang the curbs on turns do need to belly out. These include operators of tractor-trailers, buses, construction equipment, and farm machinery. However, the driver of a passenger car who starts from the center of their lane and enters the center of the lane on the side street will normally miss the curb. For this maneuver, your vehicle should be about two or three feet from the right side of the road. Before turning right, look for pedestrians crossing the street you are turning into and bicyclists passing you on the right as they attempt to proceed straight through the intersection. In some states the bicyclist has the right-of-way.[67]

"Reeling"

One trick that professional drivers use both on curves on freeways and on turns into side streets is reeling in or reeling out the wheel as the turn is made. For instance, at the beginning of a right turn, you will feel centrifugal force pushing you to the left. If you pull hard on the wheel, the centrifugal force will push your left shoulder against the car door. For this reason, the pros turn their steering wheels slightly at the very beginning of the turn. Then they gradually turn the steering wheel more to the right as they slow down. Conversely, starting from a traffic light, they may turn the wheel sharply as they start into the turn and then ease it back to the left as they gain speed. This is a more comfortable way to turn for both drivers and passengers. And it reduces the likelihood of flipping your car.

Turn Only When Space Is Available

Do not begin your turn into a side street or driveway until there is space there for your car.

Turn in Front of a Car Turning From the Oncoming Lane

When you are making a left turn, you may find that someone approaching the intersection from the opposite direction also wishes to make a left turn. You will turn in front of that car and she will turn in front of you.

Do Not Stop With Your Wheels Turned

Are you stopped at a light waiting to turn? If so, do not have your wheels turned before you begin moving again. If you are rear-ended, having your wheels turned will cause your vehicle to spin around and result in a much more serious crash. And, as mentioned earlier, if you have a manual transmission, you should consider keeping it in neutral until it is time to go.

U-Turns

Ideally, you should back into a spot to turn around so that your car is facing traffic when you reenter the highway. This is safer than backing out into an active street. To turn more safely, drive just past a side street and back slowly into it when the way is clear. Stop backing when you are all the way into the side street. Then signal and turn left. In busy cities and towns the safest way to U-turn may be to drive around the block or use a parking lot to turn.[68]

Uphills

Steep uphills can be found almost anywhere, on back roads, in hilly towns and cities, and on steep driveways. Fortunately, several years ago the auto manufacturers installed "hill holders" on their cars. These devices prevent your car from rolling backward when you stop on a steep uphill.

Climbing Lanes

Out on the freeway, you will often encounter "climbing lanes" on uphills. A climbing lane is an additional lane on the right. It is there so that slower trucks and cars do not tie up traffic in the normal lane or lanes. You should use the lane if there is a driver behind you who wishes to pass.

If a climbing lane is added to a two-lane road, then the drivers coming down hill are usually prohibited from passing by a double yellow line. See Chapter 11, "National Issues," for a potentially dangerous exception found in western states.

Some hotshot drivers will air out their big engines on these uphills, passing everyone in sight. Their reasoning may be that the police do not have their radar out in these locations. That is a false assumption, as a friend of mine found out last year.

Effect of Gravity

In one way, uphills are safer than downhills. Just as an airplane lands into the wind to slow down rapidly, so will your car slow more quickly on an uphill. This may prompt you to move a little faster on the uphill, particularly if poor driving conditions have drastically reduced your speed. If you do, please keep your speed at a safe level and beware not to exceed the speed limit.

Wide Loads

Modular homes are a commonly seen wide load on freeways. The trucks transporting these loads usually are adorned by flags and large banners. In addition, they will be both preceded and followed by smaller vehicles equipped with flashing lights and more signs. In some states, a state trooper will bring up the rear of this easily identified caravan.

As an overtaking driver, you should be aware that these loads might be twelve or more feet wide. And they can be blown from side to side if there are crosswinds. For these reasons, you should watch the load to see if it is encroaching on your lane before you attempt to pass. Next, select a straight stretch of highway for overtaking. Pass as rapidly as the speed laws allow and keep as far to the left of your lane as is safely possible. (Also see the section of this chapter entitled "Math and Physics.")

Wind

Wind conditions can put your car in extreme peril. Sharp gusts of wind can cause you to lose control if you don't have a firm grip on the wheel. Strong winds also can blow debris or sand against your windshield, thereby blinding you. In a snowstorm, wind can cause a whiteout. Listed below are a few other wind problems.

Intermittent Gusts
I encountered an unexpected wind condition on the Tappan Zee Bridge north of New York City. While crossing with my family many years ago in a light minivan, I was experiencing strong gusts of wind from the right side. These were caused by gaps between the bridge girders that threatened to blow the van into the next lane to our left or even into the oncoming lane that was two lanes over. After this experience, I always waited for a tractor-trailer to come up in the right lane. Then I kept my vehicle alongside it as we crossed the bridge and let it take the wind gusts for us.

Bow Wave from Trucks
There are some other, less-recognized effects from the wind. For instance, the fronts of large trucks create the previously discussed bow stream of wind much like the wake from a motorboat. This can push your car away from a truck when you attempt to pass. This effect was described previously in the section entitled "Trucks." If you are right behind a truck, the turbulence from its slipstream can move your vehicle from side to side.

Strategies for Driving in Strong Winds
My experience on the Tappan Zee Bridge notwithstanding, it is a good idea to keep your vehicle as far away as possible from vehicles in other lanes. If on a two-lane highway, move your car to the right side of your lane. Reduce your speed, grip the steering wheel firmly,

and avoid passing. If the wind is gusty, it will move your vehicle to one side. Use your steering wheel to compensate gently as soon as your car moves the slightest bit off course.[69]

Impact on Gas Mileage

And if you are interested in good gas mileage, know that a headwind will reduce it, especially if you are carrying a storage unit or watercraft on your roof. This is noted in the section in this chapter entitled "Energy-Saving Strategies."

Windshield Wipers

When I owned a small MG-TD English sports car, the wiper motor was mounted on the inside of the "windscreen" on the passenger side. When my motor burned out, the wipers could still be operated manually. It was thus necessary for me to have a passenger in the car whenever it rained. This experience proved to me in no uncertain terms that wipers are the one appliance whose absence makes driving in poor weather extremely difficult. However, modern wipers are very reliable and only need new blades once a year or so. Chapter 8 discusses what to do if they do fail (thankfully, today's cars lack that handle on the inside of the windshield that allows you to rotate the wipers by hand).

Some Tricks for Better Visibility

One trick already mentioned is to speed up your wipers before passing a tractor-trailer or any vehicle whose large tires and high clearance create a spray behind it. Another trick is to turn on your air conditioning if your windshield continues to fog up after you set your blower to its highest defrost setting. Also see the next chapter entitled "Winter Driving."

Bug Attacks

Springtime brings insects to our roads. Sometimes these are so thick that they can virtually cover your entire windshield. They are especially heavy towards evening and when you drive over rivers or past swampy areas. You should stop and clean your windshield (and headlights) if they obstruct your vision. The water and cloth that you carry in your car can be used, but you may want to carry paper towels and some glass cleaner as well during bug season.

CHAPTER 7 – WINTER DRIVING

Winter driving is a special skill that is needed if you live in the northern part of the United States. As such, it is worthy of a special chapter. Of course, there are cold winters and then there are the frigid winters that one often encounters in places such as Alaska, Minnesota, and northern Canada. The following text is geared toward what one might call an "ordinary" winter. Colder locales may well call for additional measures including the use of car heaters and special motor oils.

Prepare Your Car

The Checklist
For basic items, see the section entitled "Before You Drive" in Chapter 5. Several items listed there are repeated here because of their importance in preparing your car for winter.

- Check coolant for low temperature
- Check tires for wear and proper inflation
- Check wiper blades, battery, and heater for proper operation
- Mount snow tires or tires with studs if needed in your area
- Put in an ice scraper, a gallon of windshield washer fluid, and a snow shovel

Also check the coolant level. The wiper blades can be replaced with winter blades that have a rubber boot covering the arm to prevent snow and ice buildup. Batteries that are three years or older also may need replacement.[1]

Outfit Your Car with the Right Stuff

Take your cell phone (see the section entitled "Before You Drive" in Chapter 5). Here is a list of additional things that you may need to carry in the car:

- Jumper cables
- Sleeping bag
- Tow chain
- Tire chains or straps (especially for mountain travel)
- For extended travel, extra clothes and drinking water

You also may need to install a block heater and use extra-lightweight engine oil. Check with your dealer.

Add Weight for Traction

Adding weight over the rear axle is very helpful for increasing traction in pickup trucks and other rear-drive vehicles. You should check with your dealer to determine the amount of weight to add. Be sure the weight will not cause damage to you if you stop suddenly. While bags of sand are considered safer than cement blocks, both constitute a hazard. Ideally, the extra weight should be securely attached to the truck bed.

Learn to Drive on Ice

I was somewhat hesitant to tell you to learn to control a skid by finding a very large, icy parking lot (free of other vehicles and perfectly level) and actually twist the wheel at a very slow speed to initiate a skid. Then I saw a course for school bus drivers and there they were, hitting the brakes and careening over a large, icy parking lot. They do this to learn how their vehicle feels in a skid.

To initiate your skid, go slowly across the lot. As you approach the middle, slam on your brakes and see if the car skids to one side. If it does, take your foot off the gas immediately and steer in the direction of the skid. Be ready to steer in the opposite direction if your vehicle starts swerving that way. Remember, a slippery surface greatly reduces traction, so any sudden movements will break the grip between the road and your tires. Conversely, taking your foot off the gas will slow the car and let you regain traction. If you have antilock brakes, they will automatically cycle on and off as you lose traction.

Next, drive across the lot in a straight line, take your foot off the gas, and tap your brakes gently. Experiment to see how much brake pressure you can exert without skidding. Also note carefully how long it takes you to stop. It will be much longer than if you are on dry pavement. This means that you can't slam on your brakes on an icy highway. And, you must leave plenty of space between yourself and the car ahead.[2]

Deciding to Go

The most important decision you will make in winter is whether or not to leave your house. If the conditions are unsafe, you should stay at home.

Why Southern Drivers Are Smart Drivers

The news broadcasters in the northern United States love to show video clips of traffic after a snowstorm in the south. There is considerable joshing about the ineptitude of drivers in "low snow" states. Their northern cousins cannot understand how an inch of snow can tie up entire cities. Actually the southern drivers who adopt a "No go in low snow" policy are the smartest drivers around. Why? Here are a few reasons:

- They don't own warm clothes.
- They don't have experience driving on ice and snow.
- They don't have snow tires or all-wheel drive.
- The other vehicles also lack snow tires, all-wheel drive, or extra weight over the rear axle.
- Their roads are not designed for ice or heavy snow.
- Their municipality doesn't have sufficient snow removal equipment or experienced operators.

When to Stay Home

One classic case for staying home was an ice storm in Eugene, Oregon, on December 6, 2013. In one day, the city had over 250 crashes. It is a city where snows are infrequent. I was driving there several years earlier and came upon a bend on a local expressway that was glazed ice. The cars ahead of me were sliding slowly into the median. The reason that they accumulated in this one icy spot is that the highway was super-elevated more than usual to allow the heavy rains in that area to drain rapidly. The problem was that it was so steeply cross-sloped that no vehicle could hold its traction once a driver so much as tapped their brakes. In other words, the road in this low-snow climate was not designed for winter weather. As the pile of cars and trucks grew, it proved the theorem that if your car skids to a certain place, so will the next car. Fortunately there were no severe injuries because the skids and crashes were occurring at a very slow speed. I slowed beforehand, avoided using my brakes, and made it through.

Before You Leave the House

The first two things to do are check the weather and dress appropriately. If you prefer driving in shirtsleeves in winter, be sure to take enough extra clothes with you to keep you warm in case your car breaks down. If needed, shovel your driveway. And, finally, check your gas gauge. Any water in the gas line can freeze in winter, so it's best to keep the gas tank as full as possible. Dry gas can be added if it will help prevent fuel line "freeze up" on your car. Again, check with your dealer.

Start the Car

Starting a car in winter is not always a sure thing. Hopefully your car will turn over easily without having to resort to the series of steps that follow.

Frozen Locks

Having grown up in a home without a garage, I watched our family cars rust and the old Woodie actually delaminate in the dampness. As a result, I am a firm believer in the benefits that garages offer. One large benefit in winter is avoiding problems with frozen locks. If your locks do freeze, you may not even be able to get into your car. There are cans of spray for unfreezing locks. Keep one handy in your house, not your car!

People who park their vehicles outside during a snowstorm may put some duct tape over their locks if they've had freezing problems. Or, they will warm their key with their cigarette lighter or even their armpit. One thing not to do is twist the key when it won't go. A broken or twisted key is a very big problem. Other options are to enter the car through another door or, if appropriate, the rear hatch if those entrances are keyed. You may even consider leaving your car unlocked if the area is "safe."

Battery

Before turning the ignition on to start the car, make sure that all the other electrical items in the car are off so that there is a minimum drain on the battery. Be especially sure that your wipers are off. If the wipers are frozen to the windshield and they are turned on, you risk burning out your wiper motors.

Depress the Clutch

In a standard transmission car, depress the clutch when you turn the key. This takes the transmission load off the starter motor. Some cars will not let you start the car unless the clutch is depressed.

Crank the Starter for Short Periods

Continuous cranking quickly drains a battery. Instead, operate the starter with a series of short cranking periods followed by a time gap. This minimizes the drain on the battery. If you smell gas, the car is flooded. Wait a couple of minutes before you try again, then fully depress the accelerator pedal and turn the starter.

In Extreme Cold

If it's really cold, or it's at the cold end of your engine oil limits, say 20 degrees below zero Fahrenheit, you can take a few extra precautions. First, try to park in an area that is protected from the wind and drifting snow. Then, get up during the night and run the car briefly. This prevents it from locking up. In the morning, wait until the sun shines on the car so that it warms up before you try to start it. As an alternative, use a plug-in engine block heater to keep the engine warm overnight.

Jumper Cables

Finally, if it doesn't start, you'll have to use jumper cables. Have someone show you how to use jumper cables before winter arrives.

Warm Up Your Car

Today's cars do not need to be warmed up in order to drive. On some cars, the motor will start to race when first started and you have to press down and release the accelerator to return the engine to idle. Check with your dealer. You still may want to warm up your car for your personal comfort. Automatic car starters can be appealing, as long as you're very sure you won't forget from your cozy indoors that you've started the car!

Clean Your Windshield

Once your car is started, you can turn on your heater to warm the windshield. This will hasten removal of ice. The quickest way to heat the inside of the car is to leave the blower off until the engine is warm. Otherwise, the cold air that circulates through the heating system will cause the coolant to warm more slowly. If you find your side windows frosted as well, roll them down (but stop them an inch or so from the bottom to avoid getting moisture inside the door). As you roll your windows back up they should be clear.

Use All Your Senses

Everyone is familiar with the cue cards used to guide TV announcers. For driving safely in winter, you need to take advantage of all possible cues about the road surface and the weather. And, you may need to sacrifice a few creature comforts to have your senses operating at their maximum. The cues that you will need include:

Sight

A clean windshield and headlights are critical for winter driving. Slush on the road accumulates slowly on both. So you should remind yourself to periodically pull off the road and clean them.

As mentioned in the section in Chapter 6 on headlights, you should run with your headlights on in the daytime as well as at night to assist other drivers as well as yourself. During a snowstorm, your low beams will illuminate the road better than your high beams.

If you haven't cleaned the snow off your roof, you may be in for a surprise when you brake suddenly. All that snow will slide forward and completely cover your windshield, blinding you. Snow also can blind you if it comes off the roof of a car or truck in front of you; and as a result, in some places you can be fined if you are traveling on the highway with a roofload of snow.

Usually, having your defroster set on high and operating your wipers will keep your windshield from freezing. However, at a temperature just below freezing, your wipers may ice up. If so, shut them off briefly and see if the heat from your defroster is enough to keep the windshield clear. Also see the section in Chapter 6 entitled "Windshield Wipers."

Touch and Feel
You need to feel the instant that your car loses traction. You can even feel when it's close to losing traction as you become a more experienced driver. For a good sense of touch, you are better off without heavy mittens. Try to get by with bare hands or thinner gloves. You also want your feet to be able to feel if the tires start to spin or lock up during braking. For this, you are better off without humongous boots. Clodhoppers also slow you down if you have to move your foot quickly between pedals. Wear your normal shoes instead. Then, put on the boots when you get out of the car.

Hearing
Usually somewhat less important, your sense of hearing can give you a critical edge in winter. For example, a change in pavement noise can signify an icy patch. Snow that crunches provides better traction than silent snow. This is not the time to listen to the car stereo. And it certainly is not the time to talk on a cell phone or text.

On the Road

In winter, you have to concentrate on your driving much more than in the summer. As we just mentioned, the first things that you should do are turn on your headlights, turn off that stereo, and take off any heavy gloves. Phew! Now you can start driving with the assurance that you are as ready as possible.

Reduce Speed to Match Conditions
On the first traffic-free stretch of straight, level highway, run your car at no more than 15 miles per hour and gently depress the brakes to see if the surface is slippery. Adjust your speed accordingly. Remember not to stop suddenly during your trip; instead, allow extra distance for stopping. And, do not change direction suddenly, as that may cause you to skid. If there is snow on the pavement, try to keep at least one set of wheels in the tracks of

the previous vehicle. Finally, keep a safe gap between you and the vehicle ahead and *never* use speed control.

Watch for White Cars
Be on the lookout for white cars, they are extremely hard to see in winter. If you own a white car, keep your headlights on at all times.

Watch for Icy Pavement
Pavement conditions are a good reason for slowing down in winter. This goes for SUVs and all-wheel drive vehicles as well, as they are just as susceptible to skidding as other cars. As you drive, watch for high embankments or wooded areas that block the sun from the road, resulting in icy pavement. Particularly dangerous is black ice as it is difficult to see. Black ice is commonly found on roads that run near bodies of water. Bridges, bridge abutments, and overpasses also are common spots for black ice to form. Keep an eye out for pavement that is slightly darker and a little duller looking. And be aware that temperatures don't have to be below freezing for black ice to develop.[3]

Skidding
Anyone who has gone tobogganing down a slope knows that the slightest movement of passengers will cause the toboggan to spin. However, the direction that the toboggan is traveling will not change. That is what will happen to your car if it starts to skid. It will not want to change direction. To prevent skidding, you want to hold the vehicle's traction. To do this, take your foot off the accelerator and let the additional traction associated with the slowing of your vehicle help maintain a firm grip when you turn. The best way to prevent skidding is to slow down before a patch of ice. If you sense that you already are on a patch of ice, release the accelerator to increase traction. Resist the urge to slam on the brakes; that will most likely result in sending you into a spin.

Rearview Mirrors
Check the rearview mirror frequently and make sure that the driver behind you also is keeping a safe distance. If not, pull into the right lane and let him pass. Most multi-vehicle accidents in winter are rear-end collisions.

Clear Windshield
Slush is a combination of wet snow, sand, or dirt. It has a penchant for flying up from the road and attaching itself to your windshield once you are underway. The larger the gap between you and the vehicle ahead, the less your windshield will be covered with slush. However, your windshield still can be slowly obscured by slush from a car at distances of up to a quarter-mile ahead of you. Trucks are huge slush throwers. If the slush is flying,

and you still have to pass that truck, put your wipers on high first. Pickups also throw a considerable amount of slush, while the low rear bumpers on sedans make them the least guilty. Also see the section entitled "Trucks" in Chapter 6.

Right-Of-Way Goes to Uphill Traffic

This is actually a law in some states. The reason? If cars or trucks coming up a hill lose momentum, they are likely to get stuck and block the road.

Yield to Snowplows

This is a story about two acquaintances who didn't see a snowplow. There was an extremely heavy snowstorm in progress as they started down the northbound entrance ramp to Interstate 91 at Brattleboro, Vermont. The driver rolled down his window in order to see the freeway before he merged. But, he neglected to roll it back up. As his VW beetle reached the end of the ramp, a huge snowplow came by. The high blade on the front of the plow sent a mass of snow into the car, completely covering the two passengers.

If You Skidded Here, the Next Car Will Too

Three other friends of mine, including a world champion woman's Nordic ski racer, were returning home from a race under icy conditions because they "had" to be back to attend a social event. As they topped a hill on the freeway, their car lost traction and skidded onto the shoulder. As it skidded, the car turned sideways, so that it faced the road when it stopped. The driver remained in the car while one friend pushed on the right front bumper and the other pushed on the left rear. Their intention was to turn it until it was parallel to the road.

About then, a van full of people topped the hill and skidded along the exact same path, hitting the first car in the right front fender. The driver of the first car was unhurt, but the skier at the front had his leg broken in two places and the Nordic champion at the rear of the car, a woman weighing only 105 pounds, was flung 100 feet into the woods upon impact. While these two victims can now lead reasonably normal lives, their competitive careers have ended. The "lesson"? It is very important that you get away from your vehicle if it goes off the road until you are sure that another vehicle doesn't follow the same path. In this case, it may have helped to flag down other vehicles.

Whiteouts

Whiteouts are a special danger associated with winter driving. They are often caused by wind-driven snow. The snow also can be kicked up by a heavy truck or a snowplow. In this case, you simply back off of the offending vehicle. Whiteouts also can occur intermittently along open stretches of highway. You can often indentify these places by the snow that has drifted across the road. The shape of the drifts will tell you the direction of the wind. For these situations, slowing down and putting on your flashers is a good idea. You should try to look past the offending spot before you enter it to determine if the road continues straight or bends because you are likely to lose all reference points once you are in the whiteout. When that happens, you risk hitting the car in front of you or being hit by an oncoming or following car.

These conditions are so dangerous that it is best to stop your trip. If you must stop on the highway, it is best to pull as far off the road as possible, preferably into a driveway or rest area. My boss found out that just pulling to the side of the road is not good enough. He and his son were rear-ended because the following driver had no idea where the road was. My boss and his son were not seriously injured. However, the investigating officer suggested that if my boss had turned off his lights after he pulled off the road, the accident might have been prevented. The overtaking vehicle saw their taillights and thought that they were moving.

Frozen Wheel Wells

After driving in snow for a few hours, you may park your car while you visit someone. When you start driving again, and especially when you turn, your entire car may begin shaking. If this happens, check your wheel wells for frozen snow that is rubbing against your tires. This problem can be mitigated if you hose out the snow, ice, or mud caked up inside the wheel wells each time that there is a warm day.[4]

Frost Heaves

In late winter, ground under the pavement will thaw and refreeze. As it does, it expands, pushing up the pavement. This occurs frequently on rural highways and produces frost heaves. It is Mother Nature's version of a speed bump. Highway departments will identify many of these with fluorescent orange signs. However, not all will be marked. Obviously, you should slow down when going over frost heaves.

I was fortunate to see frost heaves in action when I was following a friend on a rural highway in the Adirondack Mountains in New York State. He was driving a popular model SUV. In order to provide off-road capabilities, the manufacturer installed a stiffer suspension system in this SUV. As my friend rounded a curve to the left, his car literally began to hop toward the outside of the road. By the end of the curve, his right wheels were almost in the ditch. The pavement was dry but the road surface had frost heaves. What was happening was that the suspension did not react quickly enough to the road surface. As a consequence, wheels were momentarily losing traction each time that the SUV went over a frost heave. With the loss in traction, centrifugal forces moved the car further and further to the right. My friend should have reduced his speed to avoid this.

Keep Some Cough Drops Handy

And here's something that you may not realize. As roads dry in winter, some of the leftover residue spread by highway crews may enter your car and cause throat irritation. Sucking on cough drops should alleviate any associated coughing when you take a long trip.

Surviving a Blizzard

It is just common sense to stay home when there is a snowstorm or blizzard. If, for some extraordinary reason, you must travel, go during daylight, take along a companion, and keep others informed of your route and schedule. Also stay on the main roads instead of taking back road shortcuts. The main roads are more likely to be plowed and patrolled.

If a blizzard does trap you in your car, here are some steps that you can take:[5]

1. Pull off the highway. Turn on hazard lights and hang a distress flag from the radio antenna or window.

2. Remain in your vehicle. It is where rescuers are most likely to look for you. Do not set out on foot unless you can see a building close by where you *know* you can take shelter.

3. Run the engine and heater about 10 minutes each hour to keep warm. When the engine is running, open a downwind window slightly for ventilation and periodically clear snow from the exhaust pipe. This will protect you from possible carbon monoxide poisoning.

4. Exercise to maintain body heat, but avoid overexertion. In extreme cold, use road maps, seat covers, and floor mats for insulation. Huddle with passengers and use your coat for a blanket.

5. Take turns sleeping. Keep one person awake at all times to look for rescue crews.

6. Drink fluids to avoid dehydration.

7. Be careful not to waste battery power. Balance electrical energy needs—the use of lights, heat, and radio—with supply (see item 1 above).

8. Turn on the inside light at night so work crews or rescuers can see you.

9. If stranded in a remote area, stomp large block letters in an open space spelling out HELP or SOS and line the letters with rocks or tree limbs to attract the attention of rescue personnel in aircraft.

CHAPTER 8 – EMERGENCIES

It was many years ago that I owned my MG Model TD sports car. It was really good-looking, but it seemed to need a tune-up every time that you drove it around the block. As mentioned earlier, the windshield wipers were temperamental as well, but the passenger could operate them manually so that did not pose any inconvenience until the passenger's arm tired. But one Thanksgiving I found myself in the middle of rural Pennsylvania driving towards my home in Ohio when the car appeared to run out of power. Since this was the Pennsylvania Turnpike, it seemed best to pull onto the shoulder and look under the hood. I lifted the hood and was greeted by a horizontal stream of gasoline. The electric fuel pump was pumping away, but most of the gas was shooting out a hole in the pump rather than finding its way to the spark plugs. Even a person such as me with less than a rudimentary knowledge of auto mechanics thought it best to kill the motor, sprint away from the vehicle, and wait for help.

Within the hour a tow truck showed up, attached itself to the front of the car and headed for the nearest exit. I hopped up in the cab beside the teenager who was driving it. Upon reaching the tollbooths at the exit, he informed me that his was only a Turnpike service and I would have to contract with someone else to tow it to a garage for repairs. Then he dropped my car—and put his tow truck in reverse! *Whack! Crunch!* The tiny MG took a hit to the radiator by his tow hook and was completely disabled. I was two hundred miles from home, had only $10.00 in my pocket and was not an American Automobile Association member. Nor was there any bus or train service nearby. Are you prepared for a similar dilemma? Back then hitchhiking was safe so that is how I got home. A better solution is carrying a cell phone and becoming a member of AAA or other reputable organization that provides roadside assistance.

My experience was far less serious than a crash. However, any gas leak should be treated seriously. Do not try to drive to a dealership. Instead, have the car towed. Smelling gas or seeing it on the ground means that the car can catch on fire and even explode at any time.[1]

The following are tips on a variety of other emergency situations.[2] It is recommended before reading these that you compare them very carefully to those recommended in your state's driver's manual. In all cases, it is important to think before you act. Do not panic. Your very survival may depend on your ability to stay calm and your knowledge of the best action to take.

Emergency Vehicles

If you see a police car or ambulance with flashing lights coming from either direction on an undivided highway, slow and pull to the side of the road. It is the law in most states.

Stopped Police Vehicles

If you see a police car with flashing lights along the side of the road, you should either slow down (the officer may be opening his driver side door) or move one lane to the left if that lane is unoccupied. Many states now have laws requiring that you do this. Also see the section entitled "Speed Limits" in Chapter 6.

Flat Tire

Pull far enough off the road to allow yourself room to change the tire without kneeling in the active highway lane. Stop and change the tire. If you need help, call roadside assistance. If you have a "run flat" tire, proceed at a safe speed to your dealer. If you have regular tires, it is best to learn how to change the tire before it goes flat in some remote location. You can practice this in your driveway when you first bring the car home from the dealer.

Blowout

You will hear a loud thumping and feel that you are losing control of the car. If it is a front tire, the vehicle will swerve to the side of the blowout. If it is a rear tire, the car will sway from side to side. Losing a wheel is similar to a blowout. In both cases, you should:[3]

1. Hold the steering wheel tightly and keep the vehicle going straight.
2. Take your foot off the gas pedal and allow the vehicle to slow gradually.
3. Brake gently *only* when your speed is slow enough to maintain control.
4. Use turn signals and pull well off the road.

Sudden Acceleration

On rare occasions and for various reasons, a car can accelerate by itself. But the solution is always the same:[4]

1. Apply brakes firmly; don't lift your foot from the pedal.
2. Shift to Neutral.
3. Steer to the side of the road.
4. Switch off the engine, then shift into Park.

Windshield Wipers Fail
Roll down the window and stick your head out so that you can see ahead. Then move your car well off the highway.

Hood Flies Up
Immediately slow down and position yourself so that you can look through the open area just above the dashboard. If you can't see that way, stick your head out the window. Then slow down and pull well off the road.

Disabled Car
A sign on the West Virginia Turnpike reads, "CRASH NOTICE: If No Injury, Remove Vehicle From Roadway." In other words, move your car to the side of the road. Park only where other drivers can see you when they are at least 200 feet away. Turn on your flashers or parking lights. Raise the hood and tie a white cloth to the driver's side door handle. Get out and move away from the car. Call for roadside assistance. If you have flares or reflectors, place them 200 feet in front of the car and 200 feet to the rear.[5]

Crash in Front of You
If you see a crash occurring in front of you, brake immediately and pull over if you can. For instance, if you are on an interstate and a car in front of you slowly leaves the highway, the driver may have fallen asleep. Or, you may see a cloud of dust ahead of you that is the result of a crash in progress. The momentum of a vehicle in the collision may cause it to bounce off an obstruction such as a tree or another vehicle and reenter the roadway on its side right in front of you, or cross the roadway in front of you and come to a stop on the other shoulder. If you do not brake immediately, you will collide with the vehicle as it reenters your lane. Call 911 immediately and give your milepost location. Interstates and Federal highways often have "mileposts" every two-tenths of a mile.

Brakes Fail
Your brakes may be about to fail if your brake pedal feels "spongy" or slowly sinks to the floor as you push it. If they suddenly give out you should:

1. Pump the brake pedal.
2. If it doesn't work, shift to a low gear.
3. Apply the emergency brake.
4. If on a steep downhill, look for bushes or a guardrail to sideswipe.
5. Use your horn and lights to warn others that you are out of control.
6. Look for a place to coast to a stop.
7. Once stopped, make sure your vehicle is well off the road and seek help.

As an extreme measure (which I don't recommend), you have the option of using the engine to slow you down by turning it off and leaving the car in gear. *Be very careful.* If the vehicle ignition switch locks the steering wheel when you turn off the key, you will not be able to steer, and if your power steering is off, the wheel will be extremely hard to turn.[6]

You Are Involved in a Crash

If possible, move your car to the side of the road.

Once safely stopped, move away from your car and remain calm. It is usually best to remain nearby until assistance arrives, even if a stranger offers you a ride.

If unable to open the car door, break open a window. You also may have to cut your seat belt. For these purposes, carry AAA's "Life Hammer" or an old hammer and some tin snips secured under your seat.

Alert other motorists. Do this by making your vehicle more visible. You can turn on the emergency flashers, and, if it is safe, raise the hood or tie a bright scarf to the antenna or door handle. You also can place flares or warning triangles behind the vehicle. Call your local emergency number, typically 911. Give your location as precisely as possible. Also advise the 911 operator if you believe that there are serious injuries or the possibility of a fire.

Exchange registration, driver's license, and other information with any other drivers involved in the crash in accordance with the instructions on the insurance cards provided by your auto insurer. Items you need to exchange with the other driver include:

- The other driver's name and address.
- The other driver's license number and state of issue.
- The other driver's license plate number and state of issue.
- The make, model, and year of the other vehicle.
- The damage to the other vehicle.
- The insurance company name.
- The names and addresses of any passengers.

As already mentioned, if you smell gasoline fumes, you must get away from the car quickly. Do not try to put the fire out. There's a possibility that your gas tank may explode.

If you have been in a serious crash, you or another victim may be injured and need to be strapped to a backboard to prevent permanent paralysis. Let trained emergency medical personnel extricate anyone so injured except in the case of a fire.

Stalled on Railroad Tracks

See the section in Chapter 6 entitled "Railroad Crossings."

Into the Water

Drowning in a car is something that probably has never crossed your mind. But it does happen. The advice of the experts is not to drive into any water whose depth you do not know. Water can flood your engine and render your car inoperable. If this happens, you have to decide if it is safer to stay in your car until help arrives or leave it and seek high ground. Even relatively shallow water can sweep your car away.

If your car starts to submerge, you must get out to avoid drowning. If you have power windows, lower them immediately because the water will short out the car's electrical system as the car sinks. If your power windows don't work, find an object that you can use to break out a window, preferably one that is facing up. Two choices for breaking a window are the AAA's "Life Hammer" or an old hammer of your own.

Before you break the window, release your seat belt and kick off your shoes. Do not try to crawl out immediately after breaking the window if the inrushing water prevents you. Instead, wait until the cabin is mostly full of water. There will be a remaining air pocket. This will tell you the orientation of your car because its location will be at the highest point in the cabin even if the car is upside down. Take a deep breath from the remaining air pocket, exit the car, and swim to the surface.

Vehicles with the engine in front will sink nose first so you may have to go to the back of the vehicle to get out. With windows and doors closed it may float for 3 to 10 minutes.[7]

You can't swim? Then don't take your car through even the shallowest of water.

Disabled Car in Your Lane

If you do not see it soon enough you will not have time to brake to a stop. Then you will have to steer to the right shoulder, if possible. To do this, turn the steering wheel just enough to get onto the shoulder while keeping your foot off the accelerator and brake.

Once you have passed the disabled vehicle, if there is enough space, slow gradually, and then turn the steering wheel to the left to return to the roadway. Once the front wheels are on the road, turn the wheel right to bring your vehicle back into its original path.[8]

Oncoming Car Swerves Into Your Lane

If there is a car coming head-on towards you in your lane and a crash appears likely, you have several options. Read these carefully because you will have to chose one or more and act instantaneously. A wrong choice can cost you your life. Taking the ditch is better than dying.

1. Move onto the shoulder. Move onto the shoulder to your right, if one is available, and hit your horn. Experts say that you should not move left for two reasons. First, the oncoming driver will swerve in that direction if he realizes he is in your lane. And, moving your car into the oncoming lane to your left could result in a collision with another oncoming vehicle.

If you move to the shoulder you may have two wheels on pavement and two wheels on dirt or gravel. This unbalances your car and it can skid, flip over, or shoot back across the highway. To avoid this, stay off the brake and accelerator. Look in the direction that you want to go and let the vehicle slow gradually if there is enough space. Bring your wheels that are on the dirt to within 15 inches of the pavement and look for a spot where the edge of the pavement is only a few inches higher than the dirt. Signal that you are returning to the travel lane and turn your steering wheel 1/16 to 1/8 of a turn to the left. A soon as you feel the right front tire contact the road edge, steer back to the right a little and accelerate smoothly to prevent a skid.[9]

2. Stop quickly. Apply your brakes to lessen the impact. If your car has an ABS, push hard on the brake pedal and steer in a safe direction. If your vehicle is not equipped with an ABS, push the brake pedal hard. As the vehicle begins to skid, quickly let up on the brake. Then quickly push it down again. Continue this quick pumping action until you are stopped.

3. Sideswipe. When you are faced with two very calamitous choices, the current wisdom is that it may be better to collide with a stationary object on the side of the road than with an oncoming car. If you must hit something, try to hit an object that will reduce the force of the impact such as a bush or snow bank. As a rule, try to hit with a glancing blow rather than head-on. In some circumstances you may be able to use your car to shield you from the other vehicle.

4. Speed up quickly. This may help if another car is about to hit you from the side or rear. Obviously, it is not applicable to a head-on crash situation.[10]

5. Look where you want to go. If you fixate on the car that is coming at you in your lane, you will tend to drive right into it. Instead, look at the point to the side where you want to drive your car to miss the oncoming vehicle. Then you will tend to steer to that point.[11]

Also see the sections in Chapter 4 entitled "Animals on the Road" and "Debris on the Road."

PART III
JUNIORS AND SENIORS

CHAPTER 9 – TEENAGE DRIVERS

Teens need more good advice than any other single segment of the driving population. There are about 210 crashes for every 1,000 licensed male teenage drivers. And, because of a lack of experience, the crash rate for 16-year-old drivers is more than twice that for 18- or 19-year-olds.[1] Every year, more than 3,000 teens will die from crashes, the largest single cause of death for teens. Over 350,000 will wind up in emergency rooms.[2]

The best way for a teen to learn to drive is to take a driver training course from a professional. A typical state mandate is 10 hours of seat time with a licensed instructor plus an additional six hours of observation time as a passenger in the vehicle while another student driver is behind the wheel. Seat time without a trained professional lacks common sense. The finer points of that phase of driver education (steering, shifting, proper use of roundabouts, proper speed for conditions, understanding antilock brakes vs regular brakes, to name a few) are born from details of their teaching experience, and are irreplaceable.

The Texas Transportation Institute found that teens taught by their parents were three times more likely to be involved in serious accidents than those trained in formal driver education and 2.7 times more likely to be involved in a fatal crash. The Oregon Department of Transportation found that the accident rate for teens taking formal driver education was 20 percent lower than those taking 100 hours of practice driving with their parents, and the number of traffic-related offenses was 40 percent lower.[3]

Wise moms and dads will accompany their teen for at least another 50 hours of driving after the teen completes formal driver training. This will be the time that teens need to gain the experience that hones their driving skills. It includes driving at night and in rain and winter conditions.[4]

Most Common Teen Accidents
Luckily, the American Automobile Association has recently found out why teenager driv-

ers run amuck.[5] The top three causes are overestimating their abilities, driving unbuckled, and speeding. Here is AAA's list of the top ten:

1. Overestimating their abilities.
2. Driving unbuckled.
3. Speeding.
4. Carrying rowdy passengers.
5. Indulging in wireless exchanges (phoning, texting).
6. Adjusting (tuning) music.
7. Cruising at night.
8. Drinking.
9. Getting into bad situations.
10. Taking dumb risks.

Two Speeding Teenagers

There were two newly licensed drivers in a town that I lived in recently who took it upon themselves to determine just how fast their car could go. The road they were on was straight or nearly so. As it passed the high school it curved ever so slightly to the left. The school entrance was on the right side of this curve. The school driveway crossed a three-foot ditch. In the ditch was a two-foot diameter culvert pipe. Their speeding car left the road and hit the pipe. That's where the troopers found the engine. Their bodies and the rest of the car were found scattered in a fan pattern up to 250 feet beyond the culvert. According to the accident investigators, they had to have been going well over 100 miles per hour at the time of impact. They were obviously quite unfamiliar with the steering characteristics of their compact vehicle at extreme speeds. Nor would the seat belts that they should have buckled have been of any use. They were not mature and responsible enough to start driving.

Good Laws for Teenagers

As of this writing, several states have acted on the results of the AAA survey. For example, Ohio 16-year-olds can't drive between midnight and 6 a.m. And they can carry only one passenger that is not an adult. Once they get a speeding ticket, they have to have a parent in the car. It is a very good law. Two out of three teenagers killed in crashes are passengers, not drivers. What else does the AAA recommend? Keep your ears open when your kids talk about driving. And make a contract with your teen driver that spells out the household rules and the penalties for not following them. Finally, make sure that your own driving habits are safe. Your teens will emulate your habits.[6]

Taking Extra Steps

Many parents show new drivers how to use the spare tire or change the oil. They may even see that you drive a safe car. In 1952, when I was 16, there appeared in my driveway a 1946 green Lincoln coupe (the predecessor of the two-door sedan). It cost $600.00 or almost half the price of a new car at the time. Unknown to me, my father had had a similar long-hooded car and it saved his life. It was "Linky" whom you met in our section on speeding. Dad drove it under the back of a truck that stopped in the middle of Route 27 just south of New Brunswick, New Jersey, during a very foggy evening. Linky's radiator smashed into the rear axle of the truck, which halted Dad's vehicle with the rear of the truck bed a mere two inches from the fold down windscreen. Dad bought me a similar car in the hope that it might save my life. Fortunately I never had to take advantage of that long hood.

Selecting a Car for Your Teen

Certain cars are safer for teen drivers, whether it is a family car or (how fortunate for the teen) their own. In either case, considering a new car is folly, since the chances of the car receiving a dent or worse is 1 in 4. Moderately priced, late-model, midsize cars offer a just-right combination of modest power and performance, top-notch crash scores, advanced safety features, and decent reliability scores. The Honda Accord, Ford Fusion, and Toyota Camry represent good midsize choices. Good choices in compact cars include the Subaru Forester and Honda CR-V. A tempting alternative is to buy a teen a very cheap, older car or pickup. Buying older cars is discouraged because they often lack safety technology such as side air bags, or antilock brakes that can greatly improve the odds of avoiding or surviving a crash.[7]

CHAPTER 10 – SENIOR DRIVERS

Senior drivers can have very serious driving deficiencies. Most experts agree that driving skills begin to decline at age 50. By age 75, people begin to slow down noticeably, and by age 85, the same people find it increasingly difficult to perform their usual daily activities without assistance.

In terms of driving safety, these declines translate into special needs that highway agencies are only beginning to address. And it is of huge significance for other drivers since it is estimated that by the year 2030, persons 65 and over will comprise 25 percent of our nation's drivers.[1] If you are over 50 you should watch for changes in your driving skills and adjust your driving habits in a way that allows you to continue to drive safely. If you are younger, you may wish to monitor the driving skills of the older members of your family. The following is an extensive checklist of physical impairments that you should watch for:[2]

- Decreases in cognitive performance
  - ○ Less attentiveness
  - ○ Slower reaction or response time
  - ○ Forgetfulness
- Losses in vision
  - ○ Poorer night vision
  - ○ Reduced ability to distinguish detail, especially while moving
  - ○ Smaller field of vision
  - ○ Slower glare recovery
  - ○ Less depth perception
  - ○ Slower visual search

- Hearing loss
    - Age 65 to 74: 24%
    - 75 and older: 39%
- Effects of medications
    - Blurred vision
    - Slowed reactions
    - Coordination loss
    - Appearance of being drunk
- Difficulties in driving
    - Reading traffic signs
    - Reading instrument panel
    - Merging and exiting in high-speed traffic
    - Turning head while backing

Types of Accidents

Failure to yield, following too closely, and driver inattention are the most common causes of accidents by "mature adults." In one-third of the crashes, typically those involving left turns, older drivers fail to yield. This is because they have difficulty assessing the time and space relationships of other vehicles in the traffic stream (see the section entitled "Time and Space" in Chapter 1).

Accident Frequency and Severity

After the age of 75, drivers are twice as likely to be involved in a crash. And older persons are the most vulnerable to injury in auto crashes. Compared to a 20-year-old, passengers age 65 and over are more than three times as likely to die from serious injuries suffered in a car accident.

Sign Legibility

The current sign legibility standard (a one-inch high letter is legible at 50 feet) corresponds roughly to a visual acuity of 20/25. This exceeds the visual acuity of at least 40 percent of drivers who are 65 and older. Standards for signs should be revised based on the minimum visibility distance needed by older drivers to read and react in time. This standard could be met by bigger and brighter signs, and wider use of signage. All drivers would benefit if roadway signs were improved to better meet the needs of older drivers. Until this is done, older drivers will have to plan their trips carefully and pay careful attention to advance signs. This also may mean traveling only in daylight hours or relying on a passenger to read signs and other markings. Also see the section of Chapter 5 entitled "Signs and Pavement Markings."

Improving Roadway Design

As mentioned, a left turn against traffic is one of the most difficult tasks for older drivers to perform. Judging gaps in oncoming traffic and reacting quickly to opportunities to turn makes this maneuver extremely hazardous and requires split-second timing. Older drivers have problems with both depth perception and judging the speed of approaching traffic, the two skills that are most critical for a left-turn maneuver. One thing that you may miss seeing is a fast-moving vehicle approaching from the opposite direction that turns right on red into the same lane that you are entering. For that reason, you must be extremely cautious when making these turns. When in doubt, wait for a better opening. It adds only seconds to your trip.

Pavement Markings

Roadway markings such as painted edge lines, grooves in the pavement along pavement edges and centerlines, and post-mounted markers provide essential visual and sound cues for lane positioning. Older drivers should rely on these as much as possible, especially at night or during other periods of poor visibility. These are relatively inexpensive items in state, county, and local highway agency budgets and should be provided and maintained in top condition. Also see the section of Chapter 5 entitled "Signs and Pavement Markings."

Special Laws for Older Drivers

Elderly drivers should check the rules for their state. As of this writing, Illinois requires road tests every two years for drivers over age 75. Massachusetts requires drivers over 75 to renew their licenses in person every five years. Eight states (Florida, Georgia, Maine, Maryland, Oregon, South Carolina, Utah, and Virginia) and the District of Columbia require elderly drivers to take a vision test when renewing their license. Washington, D.C., also requires a reaction test for drivers over 70 and a physician's ruling that the applicant is physically and mentally capable of driving. Nevada applicants for renewals must provide a medical report once they reach 70.[3]

Several states have less restrictive laws for older drivers. In North Carolina, drivers 60 and older are not required to parallel park during the road test. In Tennessee, drivers over age 65 do not have to renew their license!

Special Exercises

Senior drivers can improve their driving capabilities with exercises. One example is turning your head when making a lane change. This can become more difficult as flexibility and range of motion decrease with age. The Hartford Insurance Group and the Massachusetts Institute of Technology AgeLab currently offer a series of online videos that demonstrate these exercises.[4]

Future Technology

Some future technology may aid older drivers. These include "smart" headlights that adjust the range and intensity of light to improve night vision. Other technology might warn a driver if their car is straying from its lane. Some vehicles already come equipped with devices that alert drivers to obstacles in front of or behind their vehicle. Still others automatically slow a car if the driver isn't braking.[5]

Turning in the Keys

Driving has always been a symbol of independence. For some senior citizens, it is also the only way for them to remain active. Losing this independence can be earth shattering. Many older drivers have excellent driving skills, but health issues, medications, and normal physical and mental changes associated with aging can make driving risky. There is no set age when it's time to "turn in the keys." But if you think you might be at that point in your life or if your grown children are telling you as much, here are some warning signs:[6]

1. You have physical ailments or reduced strength, coordination, or flexibility that prevent you from turning the steering wheel hard.
2. You have leg or foot pain that makes it difficult to move your foot quickly from the gas pedal to the brake pedal.
3. You have pain or stiffness in your neck that makes it harder to look over your shoulder as you change lanes or to look left and right at intersections for oncoming traffic.
4. Your reaction time doesn't seem as fast as it used to be. You are slower to spot vehicles that have slowed or stopped in front of you or are emerging from side streets and driveways.
5. You are losing your ability to divide your attention among multiple activities.
6. You are on medication that impairs your reaction time. Always read the label and, if you are unsure, check with your physician as to whether you should be driving.
7. Your eyesight causes you to be extra sensitive to light, or you have blurred vision or trouble seeing in the dark.
8. Your hearing is so decreased that you don't hear emergency sirens, a honking horn, or other important cues for safe driving.
9. You get confused, angry, or flustered easily while driving.
10. You miss exits that once were second nature to take.

11. You make sudden lane changes, drift into other lanes, forget to use your turn signal, or accelerate or brake suddenly.
12. You have had a number of close calls lately.

If you have these or other concerns, discuss them honestly with an adult child or your doctor. It may be that it is not yet time to turn in your license if you make certain adjustments. For instance, you may decide to no longer drive when it is dark. You may stick to local roads. Or, you may take a companion with you to help you read road signs and find side streets, entrance ramps, and other turns that you need to make.

Whatever you do, you need to be confident that your knowledge, skills, and reflexes are up to par. You can begin by taking an online screening assessment. AAA and AARP both offer such questionnaires. AAA also offers a series of computer-based exercises to help test your physical flexibility and memory. If the assessments raise a red flag, the next step might be to get an on-the-road driving assessment from a rehabilitation center.

If a problem is identified, it might be fixable by a driving specialist. Specialists currently charge from $200.00 to $1,000.00 for a complete evaluation. Specialists can identify actions such as riding the brake that are a danger to their client and other drivers. At that point they can offer lessons to correct any deficiencies.[7]

Finally, if it is time for you to stop driving altogether, it will require some major adjustments that can make you frustrated, angry, or irritable. But it isn't the end of the world. You will save money on car ownership costs such as gas, insurance, maintenance, and registration. You might even improve your health by walking more or expand your social circle as you ride with others.[8]

PART IV
LAST THOUGHTS

CHAPTER 11 – NATIONAL ISSUES

Many years ago, all 50 of the United States adopted what is called the Uniform Traffic Code. This included changing the color of stop signs from yellow to red, adopting identical shapes and colors for each type of sign, and changing centerlines from white to yellow. The Uniform Traffic Code has been a great aid to drivers. And it has been followed by many federally regulated safety improvements to our cars, especially seat belts and air bags. Today, the Environmental Protection Agency supports energy conservation by requiring that gas mileages be listed for city and freeway driving. What more can we do?

Recommendations

Expand Seat Belt Enforcement Laws
Eighteen states still don't have primary enforcement laws that allow the police to ticket drivers solely for not buckling up. Surveys show that drivers in those states are less likely to wear their seat belts.[1]

Provide More Visibility Through the Car
Give the driver more visibility through the car ahead. It is difficult to see through some of today's cars and SUVs. It is a huge advantage for you if you can see if the driver in the car ahead of you is attentive. And seeing two cars ahead is a great help in avoiding rear-end crashes. You could see the brake lights two cars ahead instead of relying only on the brake lights of the car in front of you.

Some of the more calamitous head-on crashes occur when the car in front of you swerves out of its lane to reveal a car coming directly at you. Seeing the oncoming car through the car in front of you would give you time to move out of its path.

Another important benefit of improving back-window visibility is a better rear field-of-view. This makes cars easier and safer to back up. Reversing into unseen pedestrians has lead to many injuries and deaths for both children and the elderly. According to *Consumer Reports*, the blind zone distance between the rear bumper and an object 28 inches high can vary from 3 feet for hatchbacks to 40 feet for crew-cab pickups![2]

Increase Legroom

Lobby manufacturers and the federal government for new standards for legroom. It appears that a number of small cars offer insufficient legroom. During ordinary driving, that lack may cause your legs to cramp and your feet to hit the wrong pedal. In collisions, the cramped space leads to shattered kneecaps and compound fractures of both leg bones just above the ankle.

Adopt More Uniform Cabin Instrumentation

Despite previous efforts, cabin instrumentation is still not uniform enough to be safe. Have you ever rented a car and found that the headlight switch or shift lever is in a different location than it is on your own car? Everything doesn't have to be uniform, but the more critical controls should be, just as the brake and accelerator are in the same place today. The second that you spend looking for a control lever or button could be the second that kills you in a crash.

One example of an instrumentation problem is the turn signal lever on my minivan. It also dims or raises the headlights when pulled forward instead of to the side. I travel with my low beam headlights on all the time. When I signal for a right-hand turn I sometimes put on the high beams by mistake. This could blind oncoming drivers.

On the other hand, one thing that I particularly like about my minivan is that I am doing 55 miles per hour when the needle points to the top center of my speedometer. I need only a quick glance to see that I am driving at a legal speed. I recently rented a car whose speedometer needle pointed straight up at 80 miles per hour. It was a somewhat pretentious compact—that speedometer went all the way up to 140 miles per hour!

The compact also had poor visibility out the windshield and required you to look down between the two front seats to see what gear you were in. Its windshield wipers required you to rotate the wiper lever for various speeds rather than pulling it up or down.

Another example is the variability in the size of side-view mirrors. My small sport utility vehicle has a side-view mirror area of about 36 square inches while the area of the side-view mirrors on my minivan is 43 square inches. Obviously a large mirror is more helpful while a very small mirror may cause you to miss seeing a passing car. And there are some very small mirrors out there! I measured one that is only 16 square inches in area!

Require Daytime Headlights

All 50 states should require that all cars have their headlights on during daytime hours. This is the law in Canada. It also should apply to motorcycles and possibly even bicycles.

Require Backup Warnings

Most commercial vehicles emit a beeping sound when backing up. Cars also should have this feature, although the beeping need not be continuous or as loud.

Lower Fog Light Beams

Improve the rules for using fog lights. Some are as bright as high beam headlights. Their beams should always be directed sufficiently downward to avoid blinding oncoming drivers.

Put the Most Efficient Fuel Speed on New Car Stickers

Place the speed that yields the optimum gas mileage on new car stickers. When conditions permit, traveling at that speed will save you gas. For example, if the speed at which you get the best gas mileage is 55 miles per hour, then you should travel at that speed whenever it is safe to do so. Obviously that does not include school zones or interstates with 70-miles-per-hour posted speeds. The first is illegal, and both are dangerous because of the difference between your speed and that of other drivers.

Post the Safe Stopping Distance on New Car Stickers

Have the estimated stopping distance for emergency braking at some speed such as thirty miles per hour listed on new car stickers. The Federal Government should make sure that the stopping distance provided by the manufacturer is realistic because most drivers think they can stop in a much shorter distance. Perfectly functioning brakes may not be able to stop you in the distance that you think they can.

Add Headlight Visibility to New Car Stickers

Have a similar measure for headlights. While some states test headlight settings and their minimum brightness, it would be nice to know just how your headlights compare to those of other cars. This is especially important for elderly drivers.

Aid Elderly Drivers

To assist older drivers, adopt further traffic control measures that provide larger lettering on signs, increase the number of dedicated left-turn lanes and left-turn signals, and keep roadway markings painted.

Stiffen Penalties for Running Red Lights

The foremost need is to step up enforcement and stiffen the penalties for running red lights. With increased traffic, there are more traffic lights than ever before. This means more traffic deaths and property damage and, interestingly enough, further traffic congestion. This occurs as more and more drivers in areas where lights are run wait four seconds after the green before entering an intersection to avoid red-light runners. If the total amount of green time is 20 seconds on that approach and their delayed start takes four seconds of that time, there remain only 16 seconds of green time. This reduces the capacity of that entrance to the intersection by 20 percent!

Post Traffic Deaths or Accidents

Government transportation agencies already collect and analyze traffic death and accident data but do not share it directly with motorists. It would be extremely helpful when you approach an intersection to know how many accidents occurred there the previous year. Even more signs delineating high-accident areas would alert us to added danger.

Eliminate Dangerous Railroad Crossings

Work to eliminate dangerous railroad grade crossings in your home town. This must include new funds to build needed grade separations.

Adopt National Standards for Licensing Drivers

Over the last several decades, more and more drivers take trips to other states. For example, on a first-time vacation trip from New Hampshire to Florida, a driver passes through 10 separate states with unfamiliar laws. That is why it is so important to secure nationwide standards for licensing drivers and renewing licenses, especially those regulating youth, DWI violators, and the elderly.

And while we are at it, we should reevaluate our road tests to make sure that they include a portion dealing with today's large, multi-lane intersections. As stated earlier, while some states have tightened their restrictions on teen drivers, others have reduced driver-training requirements despite studies that show this increases accident rates. Concurrently, several states have passed legislation requiring elderly drivers to retake their road test. But would you believe that at least one state does not require that you renew your driver's license after age 65!

Adopt a Truly National Uniform Traffic Code

And, finally, we can urge our legislators to amend the National Uniform Vehicle Code and our municipal traffic ordinances so that there is more consistency. Many of the current traffic laws differ from state to state. Here is one example of how the lack of uniformity in "rules of the road" can be dangerous. Most states allow U-turns at signalized intersections on divided highways. Wisconsin does not. So, the Wisconsin resident visiting your state will not be ready for your next U-turn. If he ignores you and takes a right turn out of that crossroad at the same time that you are turning into the same lane, there will be a crash.[3] Interestingly, a sign at an Inverness, Florida, intersection reads "Right On Red Yield To U-Turns."

Another example is the treatment of no-passing zones that is discussed in the section entitled "Signs and Pavement Markings" in Chapter 5. While these discrepancies may not be as dangerous as different U-turn laws, they still may be confusing for motorists from other states. For example, you may miss the end of the no-passing zone if you go from a state that uses the pennant-shaped signs to one that doesn't.

Perhaps the most dangerous practice that I have seen occurs in at least two western states. There, motorists coming down a steep hill are permitted to pass when a two-lane road is widened to include a climbing lane for slow moving vehicles coming up the hill. With this allowed, you can have two passing vehicles coming toward each other in the same lane. The two oncoming vehicles can easily be closing at 150 miles per hour. This is 220 feet per second, the same as the takeoff speed for a jetliner. It is dangerous for a driver coming up the hill if he comes from a state where the downhill driver always has a double yellow line because the driver coming up the hill will not be looking for an oncoming vehicle in the passing lane. At these speeds the results can be disastrous.

Adoption of a more universal code will not be easy. To speed things along, the states with serious exceptions should be permitted to retain some of their unique rules and sign usage if they highlight them in their driving manuals.

Require Liability Insurance

Having adequate insurance should be a prerequisite to registering a vehicle for all drivers in all 50 states. And, if the insurance lapses, there should be an automatic process for revoking that registration. See the section entitled "Uninsured Motorists" in Chapter 5.

Support Good Highways

In a recent editorial, Thomas D. Kinley, president of the American Automobile Association of Northern New England wrote the following:

> For the past 20 years, our nation has underinvested in its roads, highways, bridges, and transit systems. Recent reports indicate huge needs for repairing, rehabilitating, and expanding the transportation system. The cost of addressing this problem over the next five years has been estimated at $1.25 trillion— more than twice current spending levels. [4]

Cutting highway maintenance budgets has been one of the favorite remedies proposed to balance federal, state, and local budgets. However, neglected highways are unsafe. And they exact a heavy hidden tax on citizens. The tax comes in the form of increased crashes, broken shocks, ruined wheel bearings, compromised tires, worn springs, dangerous misalignments, and a host of other damage to our cars. In total, these require families to retire their autos or trucks far earlier than they would normally do. As a neighbor put it at our town meeting, "I don't mind going into the potholes, but when I have to shift to low to get out, I've got a problem." He will not be the only one. Every citizen and business within the impacted jurisdiction will incur a significant increase in their personal transportation costs, an increase that is often far greater than the amount of taxes that budget cuts in highway maintenance will save. So, *please* support highway budgets in your area.

CHAPTER 12 – CONCLUSIONS

Justifying Additional Driver Knowledge and Training

This book is neither complete nor exhaustive in its presentation of advanced driving techniques. Today, more and more driver education programs are not just teaching the basic physical skills of operating a car, but are emphasizing cognitive skills as well, such as perception, reasoning, and judgment. As a proactive driver, it is important that you constantly update and expand your own knowledge and skills. Updating skills already is an absolute necessity for professionals in fields as varied as automotive repair, computer science, medicine, and a host of other occupations. Here are some additional sources of driver education information as this intriguing field of human activity rushes into today's period of rapid technological change:

- The first source of information is your state's driver's manual. This document is designed to provide an understanding of the basic traffic laws and driving practices needed to obtain an operator's license. Most importantly, it provides the latest recommendations for avoiding crashes.

- Those readers interested in an easily readable and well-illustrated textbook with plenty of practical tips on how to drive should consider *Responsible Driving*, a 432-page soft-cover book published by McGraw Hill in 2000. Sponsored by the American Automobile Association, it draws on the experience and current thinking of experts across the country.

- For new drivers who want to know more about the ins and outs of driving, there is *The Driving Book,* written by Karen Gravelle and illustrated by Helen Flook. Published by Walker Publishing Company in 2005, this 170-page book presents easy-to-read text and illustrations for the beginning driver.

- For those in the driver education field, the American Driver Training and Safety Education Association offers its *ADTSEA Driver Training Curriculum*

2.0. This document is rich in detailed procedures for driver educators. It can be obtained from ADTSEA at 1434 Trim Tree Road, Indiana, PA 15701 (adtsea.org).

- Those interested in the psychology of driving might try *Traffic: Why We Drive the Way We Do*, by Tom Vanderbilt. This intriguing and well-researched 402-page book was published by Random House in 2009.

Being a Proactive Driver

As a proactive driver I want you to be completely and absolutely focused on the world outside the cabin of your vehicle. I want you to be alert and constantly scouting ahead. Sure, I have said in page after page that this or that situation is dangerous. But the vast majority of the cited situations are dangerous only if you are unaware of their underlying hazards and pitfalls. When done well and with proper knowledge, driving becomes an extremely pleasurable experience. And it will be a constant source of pride that you can share with other proactive drivers.

Even the Best Make Mistakes

Proactive drivers are realists. Deep down, they know that someday they will accidently make a big mistake. Even the very best of drivers may exit their driveway without looking, roll a stop sign, or make a left turn in front of an oncoming car. What they are hoping is that when they do, the other driver will be proactive as well and there will be no crash.

The Joy of Driving

Are you now wondering why all those people in other autos always want to be somewhere else? Why do they hold a cell phone to their ear as they turn through a busy intersection? Wouldn't it be wonderful if they found driving their car to be as pleasurable and relaxing an experience as you do? After all, over the course of their lifetime they will drive enough miles to go to the moon and back, plus some.

You're not the only one. A neighboring dairyman drives around our small town, looking at other farms. What he sees in their fields helps him decide when to plant and when to harvest. Another neighbor drives over-the-road trucks. He's tried other jobs but he always goes back to his first love, the open highway. Our children are honing their powers of observation on long vacation drives, enthusiastically playing "Auto Bingo." An elderly couple that we know goes for a drive in the early evening. At sunset, they stop on a nearby hill and step from their car just as they did when they were teenage sweethearts. Arm in arm they gaze in rapture at the brilliant sunset. Yes, as a nation, many of us still "LUV-2-DRYV." What a glorious way to see our neighborhood and our country!

APPENDIX 1

Rules of Three: The List

CHAPTER 1
The three steps for proactive driving are scouting, deciding, and acting.

CHAPTER 2
Proactive drivers minimize perception, reaction, and braking time. These very specific actions are directly associated with scouting, deciding, and acting, respectively.

Proactive drivers strive to maintain a gap of at least three seconds between their car and the car that they are following.

Proactive drivers use all three of the senses available to them for operating a car; seeing, hearing, and feeling.

Proactive drivers know that just one second of inattention can cause an accident while three seconds of inattention is a virtual guarantee that a crash will happen.

Proactive drivers stay home when there are three or more circumstances beyond their control that make driving unsafe.

Proactive drivers know that three speeding tickets result in a loss of license.

CHAPTER 5
Proactive drivers stop, look, and listen before crossing railroad tracks.

Proactive drivers wait three seconds before going through a traffic light, if they live in an area where motorists run red lights.

Proactive drivers activate their turn signals three seconds before they turn.

APPENDIX 2

Other Crash-Free Driving Concepts

The research for this book brought to light several other crash-free driving concepts. Like proactive driving, they offer specific strategies for beginning drivers who wish to practice defensive driving more effectively. The first of these corresponds quite closely to the proactive driver's first rule of three: scouting, deciding, and acting. It is the "SEE" system advocated by the American Driver Training and Safety Education Association:[1]

1. **S**earch for changes to the path of travel and line of sight and identify high-risk situations.
2. **E**valuate methods to reduce driver risk in identified situations, evaluate divided-attention tasks needed, and understand the consequences associated with driver behaviors and collision factors.
3. **E**xecute appropriate speed and position adjustments accompanied by appropriate communication.

Another excellent example is the "Smith System: Five Safety Keys to Crash-Free Driving":[2]

1. Aim high in steering—don't look down your fender or hood but ahead at the middle of your driving lane.
2. Get the overall picture—look ahead a full block in town and half a mile ahead outside of town. You want to see everything in the space you are moving into, along with the vehicles and bicyclists you see ahead of you.
3. Keep your eyes moving—don't look at one thing. Look ahead, look at the sides, and look in your rearview mirror.
4. Leave yourself an out—things may happen that you don't plan. Keep plenty of space between you and the motor vehicle or bicyclist ahead of you.
5. Make sure they know you are there—don't take for granted that others see your vehicle. Tap your horn or flick your headlights up and down if you need to. Don't blast your horn, especially at bicyclists or horseback riders. You could startle them and cause a crash.

A third example is the IPDE process:[3]

1. **I**dentify: Use visual search patterns to identify open and closed zones, specific clues, other users, roadway features and conditions, and traffic controls.
2. **P**redict: Use knowledge, judgment, and experience to predict actions of other users, speed, direction, control, and points of conflict.
3. **D**ecide: Decide to use one or more actions to change or maintain speed, change direction, or communicate.
4. **E**xecute: Execute your decisions to control speed, steer, communicate, and combine actions.

NOTES

Foreword

1. Larry Copeland "In a Sharp Trend Reversal, Highway Fatalities Rise," *USA Today* (May 3, 2013).

Chapter 1—Introduction

1. "Highway Statistics: 2003," (U.S. Department of Transportation, Federal Highway Administration, Washington, D.C: 2004).
2. Survey on Speeding and Unsafe Driving, *ITE Journal* (April, 1999): 24.
3. "Defensive Driving," en.wikipedia.org.
4. Carol Caldas and David M. Scuro, "The Graying of America," unpublished paper, (The Port Authority of New York and New Jersey, January, 1991).

Chapter 2—The Proactive Driver

1. *State of New Hampshire Driver's Manual* (Department of Safety, Division of Motor Vehicles, August, 2006), 39.
2. Theodore M. Matson, W. S. Smith, and F. W. Hurd, *Traffic Engineering*, (McGraw-Hill, 1955), 23. Based on experiments conducted by the Massachusetts Institute of Technology.

Chapter 3—Reading Other Drivers

1. F. T., *The Old Farmer's Almanac* (Yankee Publishing, 2008), 252. The author credits www.insurance.com with reports of claims processed by the Churchill Company.

Chapter 4—The Distracted Driver

1. Joseph B. White, "When Cellphone Bans Don't Curb Crashes," the *Wall Street Journal* (February 3, 2010).
2. "Firm Hit For Lobbying Against Cell Phone Bans," the *Keene Sentinel* (July 11, 2010), B-4.
3. Tom Vanderbilt, *Traffic: Why We Drive the Way We Do*, (Vintage Books, 2009), 81.
4. "Firm Hit For Lobbying Against Cell Phone Bans," the *Keene Sentinel* (July 11, 2010), B-4.
5. "Texting While Driving Is Unsafe," the *Keene Sentinel* (July 28, 2009).

Chapter 5—Before You Go

1. "Did You Know?" *Consumer Reports* (June, 2007): 49.
2. "Quick Fixes for a Flat," *Consumer Reports* (January, 2014): 49.
3. American Automobile Association, *Responsible Driving* (McGraw Hill, 2006), 85–86.
4. Ibid.
5. Bob Johnston, "Fact or Fiction? Passenger Trains 'Lose' Money and Highways Don't," *Trains* (July, 2009): 29; Theodore M. Matson, W. S. Smith, and F. W. Hurd, *Traffic Engineering*, (McGraw-Hill, 1955), 183–184.
6. Roger Cheng, "Beyond Simple Driving Directions," the *Wall Street Journal*, (February 17, 2009): R-4.
7. Ibid.
8. Walter S. Mossberg, "These Apps Help Users of iPhones Find Their Way," the *Wall Street Journal* (September 10, 2009).
9. "Used Car's Navigation System Contains Too Much Information," the *Keene Sentinel* (April 11, 2010), B-4.
10. Edward V. Rickenbacker, *Rickenbacker: An Autobiography* (Prentice Hall, 1968), 100.
11. Ibid., 56.
12. "A Mirror Adjustment Can Make a Difference," *Oneonta Daily Star*, (April 18, 1995).
13. Hammacher Schlemmer catalog, (Spring, 2010), 5.
14. Tom Vanderbilt, *Traffic: Why We Drive the Way We Do*, (Vintage Books, 2009), 14.
15. "Ask Our Experts," *Consumer Reports*, (October, 2013), p. 5.
16. "NYC Drivers Named America's Most Aggressive," www.msnbc.com, [June 16, 2009]. Based on telephone survey of 2,518 people by Affinion Group, as reported by Reuters.
17. Scott McCartney, "My Rental Car Has How Many Miles?" the *Wall Street Journal*, (August 29, 2013): D-1.
18. Ibid.
19. Ken Thomas, "Economy Pulls Highway Deaths Back To Levels Last Seen In 1960s," the *Keene Sentinel* (April 6, 2009).

20. "Safety Restraints," *ADTSEA Driver Education Curriculum* 2.0 (American Driver Training and Safety Education Association, 2010).

21. Robert Schaller, "Secure Loose Objects!" www.roadtripamerica.com [August 6, 2008].

22. *Vermont Driver's Manual* (State of Vermont Department of Motor Vehicles, Summer, 2008), 58.

23. *Road Signs, Signals and Markings*, The American Automobile Association (May, 1993). 16-page pamphlet.

24. *Tire Maintenance, Safety and Warranty Manual* (Bridgestone/Firestone, July, 2007), 3.

25. "Run-flat Tires," *Consumer Reports* (June, 2007), 49.

26. "Get Up to Speed on Tires," *Consumer Reports*, November, 2009, p. 50.

27. Robert A Dougherty, "Bodily Injury Liability Insurance," Tampa, Florida (March 18, 2009), 1. Robert Dougherty's firm specializes in personal injury law.

Chapter 6—When You Are Driving

1. Robert Schaller, "Practice Animal Avoidance!" www.roadtripamerica.com [August 6, 2008].

2. "Be Careful Out There; You Might See A Deer," the *Keene Sentinel* (September 8, 2008), 13.

3. *Vermont Driver's Manual*, State of Vermont Department of Motor Vehicles (Summer, 2008), 68–69.

4. Pamphlet, (New Hampshire Association for the Blind, 2008).

5. American Automobile Association, *Responsible Driving*, (McGraw-Hill, 2006), 297.

6. Ibid., 260.

7. *Forester '05 Owner's Manual*, (Tokyo, Japan: Fuji Heavy Industries Ltd., 2005) 7–22.

8. "Installing and Using Child Safety Seats and Booster Seats" (Children's Hospital of The King's Daughters, April 1, 2009) 1–3. www.chkd.org.

9. Ibid.

10. Ibid.

11. Ibid.

12. "Car Seats Update," *Consumer Reports* (October, 2007), 48–49.

13. "Defensive Driving Script," *AgSafe* (National Ag Safety Database, January 29, 2009).

14. Robert Schaller, "Keep Your Child Safe in the Center," www.roadtripamerica.com [August 6, 2008].

15. "Child Safety Seat Information," Children's Hospital of The King's Daughters, (April 1, 2009), 1–2. www.chkd.org.

16. "Volvo's Latest Safety Feature," *Consumer Reports* (September, 2009): 60.

17. Robert B. Thomas, *The Old Farmer's Almanac* (Yankee Publishing, 2006), 225.

18. Edward V. Rickenbacker, *Rickenbacker: An Autobiography* (Prentice Hall, 1968), 51–52.

19. "Why Don't We Drive On The Same Side Of The Road Around The World?" www.i18guy.com [February 11, 2009], 6–10.

20. "Impaired Driving" (Bureau of Highway Safety, State of Maine, 2010), 1. Brochure.

21. "Maine's OUI Laws Explained" (Bureau of Highway Safety, State of Maine, 2010), 2.

22. "Impaired Driving," (Bureau of Highway Safety, State of Maine, 2010), 2. Brochure.

23. Ask Ann Landers, *Oneonta Daily Star* (July 10, 1997): 18.

24. Joseph B. White, "Key to Next Push for Safer Driving: Technology," the *Wall Street Journal* (January 26, 2011): D-2.

25. "Dust Storms," *Travel Tips*, Arizona Department of Public Safety, www.azdps.gov [December, 2013].

26. "Top-Mileage Hybrid Sedans Are Fords," the *Keene Sentinel* (August 23, 2009): E-1.

27. A. J. Miranda, "Pain Relief: Some Tips on Saving Money at the Pump," the *Wall Street Journal* (September 15, 2008): R–2; Matthew K. C. McKenzie, "Saving Fuel Safely: Choose the Right Techniques," *Northern New England Journey* (Northern New England AAA, November/December 2008): 4.

28. *State Of New Hampshire Driver's Manual* Department of Safety, Division of Motor Vehicles, August, 2006), 82.

29. Ibid.

30. Joseph B. White, "The Back-Seat Driver in Your Dashboard," the *Wall Street Journal* (October 26, 2011), D-3.

31. Tiffany Briggs, "Farm Equipment Is on the Region's Roads Again," the *Keene Sentinel*, (May 12, 2010): 9.

32. "Car Talk" (National Public Radio: May 28, 2011).

33. Peter Bohr, "At a Premium, Here's How to Know What Grade of Gas to Use in Your Car," *Northern New England Journey* (Northern New England AAA, January/February 2009).

34. "Myths at the Gas Pump," *Consumer Reports* (August, 2012): 55.

35. Ibid.

36. Various midday surveys of New Hampshire state highways by the author.

37. Robert Schaller, "Know When to Use Your Headlights!" www.roadtripamerica.com, [August 6, 2008].

38. Robert Schaller, "Rule 29: Check for Hydroplaning!" www.roadtripamerica.com [August 6, 2008].

39. Robert Schaller, "Beware of Intersections," www.roadtripamerica.com, [August 6, 2008].

40. Charles-Marie Gariel, "De la regle à adopter en cas de rencontre sur deux routes qui se croisent," *Revue Mensuelle* (Touring-Club de France, July, 1896): 246–247.

41. E. B. Lefferts, "Giving Man on Left Right of Way," *National Safety News* (December 1922): 40. My thanks to Kenneth Todd for unearthing these references for his letter to the editor of the August, 2008, *ITE Journal*.

42. "Subaru & Safety: A Matter of Control," *Subaru Drive Magazine* (Fall, 1997), 9.

43. *Vermont Driver's Manual* (State of Vermont Department of Motor Vehicles, Summer, 2008), 40.

44. Interview with Roger Henry, Rexford, New York, May 25, 2008.

45. William M. Bulkeley, "Cameras to Catch Traffic Scofflaws Spark New Kind of Road Rage," the *Wall Street Journal*, (March, 2009): A-1, A-10.

46. Peter Hessler, *Country Driving*, Harper Perennial (2011), 78.

47. "Trains Top Ten States for Grade-Crossing Collisions," *Trains*, (August, 1995): 17. Figures are from 1994 Federal Railroad Administration grade-crossing accident statistics.

48. *State Of New Hampshire Driver's Manual*, (Department of Safety, Division of Motor Vehicles, August, 2006), 59.

49. American Automobile Association, *Responsible Driving* (McGraw Hill, 2006).

50. "NYC Drivers Named America's Most Aggressive," www.msnbc.com [June 16, 2009]. Based on telephone survey of 2,518 people by Affinion Group, as reported by Reuters.

51. "Steer Clear of Aggressive Driving" (New York State Governor's Traffic Safety Committee, May, 1998). Handout at New York State Department of Motor Vehicle offices.

52. *Vermont Driver's Manual*, State of Vermont Department of Motor Vehicles (Summer, 2008), 34.

53. "What Keeps Drivers Awake? Hint: John Q. Public Is Wrong," *Progress Report*, AAA Foundation for Traffic Safety (July-August 1998): 2.

54. P. J. O'Rourke, *Driving Like Crazy*, Atlantic Monthly Press (2009), 196.

55. Jeff Gulden and Reid Ewing, "New Traffic Calming Device of Choice," *ITE Journal*, (December, 2009): 26–29.

56. "Road Speed Limits in the United Kingdom," en.wikipedia.org.

57. "Can't Drive 55? Try Texas," *Keene Sentinel*, (September 7, 2012).

58. www.autoblog.com [December 26, 2013].

59. "Speed Limits," and "The Interstate Highway System," en.wikipedia.org.

60. Sam Ambuelsamid, "Swedish Man May Pay Largest Speeding Fine Ever," www.autoblog.com [December 26, 2013]

61.Daven Hiskey, "The First Speeding Infraction in the U.S. Was Committed by a New York City Taxi Driver in an Electric Car on May 20, 1899, " www.todayifoundout.com [May 20, 2011].

62. "Changing Weather and Conditions of Visibility," *Driver Education Classroom and In-Car Instruction*, Unit 7-5, American Driver Training and Safety Education Association, (2010), 1.

63. "Surviving a Natural Disaster," *Health Quarterly* (Cheshire Medical Center Dartmouth-Hitchcock Keene, Winter, 2010): 2.

64. *Vermont Driver's Manual* (State of Vermont Department of Motor Vehicles, Summer, 2008), 72–73.

65. Ibid., 73.

66. "Car Talk" (National Public Radio, December 12, 2009).

67. *Vermont Driver's Manual* (State of Vermont Department of Motor Vehicles, Summer, 2008), 32.

68. Ibid., 36–37.

69. *Handbook Plus*, (Propulsion International Inc., 1999), 13.8–13.9.

Chapter 7—Winter Driving

1. "Winterizing," *Subaru Drive Magazine* (Winter, 2010), 24.

2. Victoria Miller, "How To Drive On Black Ice," www.howtodothings.com/automotive/ [January 31, 2009].

3. Ibid.

4. "Get Ready for Winter," *Northern New England Journey* (Northern New England AAA, November/December 2010), 12.

5. *Vermont Driver's Manual*, (State of Vermont Department of Motor Vehicles, Summer, 2008), 54.

Chapter 8—Emergencies

1. Tom Hartshorn, "Turn the Car Off," *Consumer Reports* (October, 2013): 5.

2. *State Of New Hampshire Driver's Manual*, (Department of Safety, Division of Motor Vehicles, August, 2006).

3. Ibid., 53–54.

4. "Surviving the Worst-Case Scenarios," *Consumer Reports* (September, 2010), 48.

5. *State Of New Hampshire Driver's Manual*, (Department of Safety, Division of Motor Vehicles, August, 2006), 60.

6. Ibid., 56.

7. Ibid., 58; *Drive Right* (Prentice Hall, 2007), 280.

8. *State Of New Hampshire Driver's Manual*, (Department of Safety, Division of Motor Vehicles, August, 2006), 57.

9. American Automobile Association, *Responsible Driving* (McGraw Hill, 2006), 298–299.

10. Tom Vanderbilt, *Traffic: Why We Drive the Way We Do*, (Vintage Books, 2009), 279.

11. American Automobile Association, *Responsible Driving* (McGraw Hill, 2006), 298.

Chapter 9—Teenage Drivers

1. Amy Dickinson, "Riding in Cars with Girls," *Time*, (January 21, 2002), 145.

2. "10 Keys to Safer Teen Driving," *Northern New England Journey* (Northern New England AAA, November/December 2011), 22–23.

3. "Eyes on the Road," the *Keene Sentinel* (January 30, 2012), 4.

4. Louise Farr, "Teens Behind the Wheel," *Ladies Home Journal* (April, 2009), 161–164.

5. Joseph D. Younger, "The 10 Deadliest Mistakes Teen Drivers Make," *Car and Travel*, (American Automobile Association, March, 2007), 14–17.

6. Alan Johnson, "Teenage Drivers Get New Limits" *The Columbus Dispatch*, April 1, 2007, 1.

7. Joseph B. White, "The Top Cars for Teens: Better Safe Than Sporty," the *Wall Street Journal*, (April 6, 2011).

Chapter 10—Senior Drivers

1. Carol Caldas and David M. Scuro "The Graying of America," unpublished paper (the Port Authority of New York and New Jersey, January, 1991).

2. Ibid.

3. Sarah Palermo, "Several States Put Older Drivers to Test," the *Keene Sentinel* (January 2, 2011): A-5.

4. Alina Tugend, "An Alternative to Giving Up the Car Keys," the *New York Times* (December 13, 2013).

5. Ibid.

6. Philip Shishkin, "Crashes Fuel Debate on Rules for Older Drivers," the *Wall Street Journal* (July 9, 2009): D-1, D-4.

7. Alina Tugend, "An Alternative to Giving Up the Car Keys," the *New York Times* (December 13, 2013).

8. Lori Catozzi, "Senior Driving And The Transition To The Passenger Seat," *Monadnock Shopper News* (September 5, 2012).

Chapter 11—National Issues

1. "Crash Course on Safety," *Consumer Reports* (October, 2013): 48–49.

2. "Best and Worst Vehicle Blind Zones, and the Role of Rear-View Cameras," www.consumerreports.org [January 28, 2011].

3. David A. Kuemmel, P.E., "Theodore M. Matson Memorial Award: Uniform Traffic Control and Uniform Vehicle Codes: A 55-Year Perspective," *ITE Journal* (October, 2008): 26–29.

4. Thomas D. Kinley, "Running on Empty," *Northern New England Journey* (Northern New England AAA, July/August, 2009): 4.

Appendix 3—Other Crash-Free Driving Concepts

1. *National Driver Development Standards* (American Driver Training and Safety Education Association, 2006), 4.

2. *Vermont Driver's Manual* (State of Vermont Department of Motor Vehicles, Summer, 2008), 58–59.

3. *Drive Right* (Prentice Hall, 2007), 63.